SUSS

MURDER
CASEBOOK

Other counties in this series include:

Essex
Lancashire
Shropshire

SUSSEX
MURDER CASEBOOK

RUPERT TAYLOR

COUNTRYSIDE BOOKS
NEWBURY · BERKSHIRE

COUNTRYSIDE BOOKS
3 Catherine Road
Newbury, Berkshire

ISBN 185306 311 8

Produced through MRM Associates Ltd., Reading
Typeset by Paragon Typesetters, Queensferry
Printed by Woolnough Bookbinding, Irthlingborough

Contents

1

THE BODY IN
THE SHINGLE

THE MURDER OF IRENE MUNRO AT THE CRUMBLES,
AUGUST 1920

The discovery made by a small boy playing on the shingle east of Eastbourne on the morning of Friday, 20th August 1920 probably put him off beaches for a long time.

As he crunched along The Crumbles, the long and desolate area of coast stretching to Pevensey Bay, he saw a human foot protruding from the pebbles. Further investigation revealed a bloody corpse on the end of it. The youngster screamed his way back into town to raise the alarm.

It needed no great feats of detection for the police to realise that the woman inexpertly buried under the shingle had been savagely battered about the head, and the bloody lump of stone beside her was the murder weapon. The only motive for the attack appeared to be that her handbag was missing.

By early evening, boarding house owners Mr and Mrs Wynniatt stood in the mortuary over the lifeless body of the young tenant they had earlier reported missing. Despite the difficulty of recognising her mutilated face, a tearful Mrs Wynniatt confirmed the identity of the victim by her green coat. She was Irene Munro, down in Eastbourne on holiday and only 17 years old.

She had been very much the innocent abroad on the first great adventure of her life. Her mother, in service as a housekeeper in South Kensington, must have had misgivings about letting young Irene come south on her own but she respected her daughter's independence and polite refusal to accompany her on Mrs Munro's own holiday – a visit to Scotland.

It was a cheerful Irene who presented herself on the threshold of the Wynniatts' establishment at 393 Seaside, Eastbourne, on 16th August. After paying her £1 deposit and settling into her room, she set off for the promenade. She was enjoying her freedom and, perhaps, harbouring wistful thoughts of a holiday romance away from parental ties. She bought six postcards, sending one to her mother and the others to friends: 'Weather absolutely gorgeous...wish you were down here.'

She also replied to a letter from Mrs Munro, which established that on the evening after her arrival, Tuesday, she went on a ramble to Beachy Head where she got lost. On Wednesday she walked to Pevensey, some five miles away, and back again. Romance must have seemed a long way off.

Maybe she wanted to help things along a little. On Thursday she went into a seaside pub and ordered herself a drink – a daring thing for a lone woman to do in 1920, especially one so young. She found male company soon enough in the shape of two young men who introduced themselves as Jack and Bill. One was about her age and the other a little older, and both were sufficiently charming for Irene to promise to meet them again that afternoon after she had been back to her boarding house for lunch.

She took considerable trouble with her appearance for Jack and Bill, dressing to the nines in her Sunday-best green coat and gaily setting out at 3 pm for her rendezvous outside the Archery Tavern.

From here, Irene and her two companions walked eastward out of the town in the direction of The Crumbles. The trio made enough of an impression on William Putland and his pal Frederick Wells that they decided to follow them 'for a lark' and see what they got up to. When it became clear that they were not getting up to anything, the two friends abandoned their furtive surveillance and returned to the pleasures of Eastbourne at the height of the holiday season.

Irene, Jack and Bill were also noticed by a gang of workmen resting in a disused carriage from their labours on the coastal railway line. They watched the young woman and her escorts until they were out of sight. It was the last time she was seen alive – except by Jack and Bill, whose motives for their visit to the shingle that afternoon were not as dreamily romantic as those of the innocent young holidaymaker they accompanied.

Later, when they were condemned to death, the pair were to turn on each other and pass the blame for Irene Munro's murder. What was clear was that at some stage, when they were well away from prying eyes, the teenager was ferociously bludgeoned with a large stone and buried under shingle, hastily heaped over the body to hide it. The pair kept her handbag.

Scotland Yard's Detective Chief Inspector Mercer soon found the witnesses he needed to identify Irene's last companions as Jack Alfred Field and William Thomas Gray, local lads with bad reputations. Field, aged 19, was unemployed and had a criminal record. Gray, born in South Africa, was 29, married and formerly a soldier but now, like Field, living off state benefit.

The case against them was overwhelming when the pair appeared in the dock at Lewes Assizes on 13th December. Just to inject further horror into the minds of the jurors, it was Sir Bernard Spilsbury's opinion that after her burial Irene 'probably survived a short time –

9

possibly half an hour, but would be deeply unconscious all the time. Death might have been accelerated by the weight of shingle on the body compressing the chest. Thus death may have been due to the combined effects of shock, loss of blood and asphyxia.'

Field made a spirited attempt to establish an alibi for himself, but it was futile and the jury returned verdicts of guilty on both men. Mr Justice Avory observed, 'The defence you concocted has been demonstrated to be untrue . . . you must now prepare yourselves to undergo the penalty which the law enacts for such a crime as you have committed.' Jack and Bill, the likely lads of the public bar, were hanged at Wandsworth prison on the morning of 4th February 1921.

Locals would often speak of a ghost which haunted the windswept Crumbles before the widespread development of the area in recent years. It was the spirit, they said, of the unhappy Irene Munro, and it was not to be the last time a woman met a violent death here.

2

THE CRUMBLES MURDER

THE MURDER OF EMILY KAYE AT EASTBOURNE, APRIL 1924

Miss Ethel Duncan would surely have politely refused Patrick Mahon's invitation to a weekend of fun if she had any inkling of what the seaside bungalow contained. In the bedroom next door to the one in which she was entertained by Mr Mahon was a cabin trunk containing the dismembered body of a woman who, only two or three nights before, had been cavorting in the same bed. Miss Duncan escaped the grisly fate of the previous guest that Easter of 1924.

Patrick Mahon was a handsome 34 year old and worked as a salesman. He was notorious as a womaniser with a string of love affairs behind him. In 1916 he had been jailed for breaking into a bank and stunning a maidservant with a hammer (he had waited for her to regain consciousness and then kissed and fondled her, begging forgiveness for the attack). His wife was the forgiving kind and when he had finished his sentence she recommended him for his job with the firm where she worked at Sunbury.

In 1924 Mrs Mahon finally became suspicious about the activities of her philandering husband. Mauverneen Mahon alerted the police after finding a cloakroom ticket in one of her husband's pockets. The police presented it at the left luggage department at Waterloo station and were given a bag which, when prised open, was found to

The charmer – Patrick Mahon.

The murder victim – Emily Beilby Kaye.

contain articles of women's silk underclothing, which appeared to be bloodstained, and a knife. The police put the ticket and the bag back and lay in wait for whoever should come to claim it.

Soon after six o'clock that evening Patrick Mahon, using the name Waller, presented the ticket and was invited by Detective Chief Inspector Percy Savage to accompany him to Scotland Yard. The contents of the bag were turned out: a torn pair of silk bloomers, two pieces of new white silk, a blue silk scarf and a large cook's knife, all stained with blood and grease. There was also a brown canvas racket bag which bore the intials 'EBK'. Mahon, dressed in a well made brown suit, his dark curly hair attractively tinged with grey, said, 'I'm fond of dogs. I suppose I've carried home meat for dogs in it.'

The explanation did not satisfy Savage, who waited with patience until eleven o'clock when Mahon calmly described his ten month affair with a woman who worked as a clerk in the City, their four days together at a bungalow near Eastbourne which ended in a violent quarrel, and her tragic death. He had hit her a glancing blow with an axe, said Mahon, and she was fatally injured after her head fell against an iron coal scuttle.

In his panic, he told the inspector, he had bought a knife and a saw and severed the woman's legs and head and stuffed the various parts into a trunk.

Still in a level, well spoken voice, Mahon described how he later returned to the bungalow from London and burned the head, feet and legs in the sitting room grate. Later again, he returned to cut up the torso and arms, boiling some in a large pot at the bungalow and wrapping up smaller portions in brown paper and throwing them out of trains. Some of the flesh had been wrapped in the bloodstained clothing found in the bag. At the end of his macabre statement, albeit not an unreasonable defence against pre-meditated murder, he finally gave the name of the dead woman, Emily Beilby Kaye.

Police went straight to the bungalow, standing on the lonely and windswept stretch of shingle between Eastbourne and Pevensey Bay known as The Crumbles. The building was called the Officer's House because it had previously been the home of the officer in charge of the coastguard station.

There were roses round the door, but when the police went inside the stench was almost unbearable. The scene, too, was ghastly. There were burned bones in the grates in the dining room and sitting room; a saucepan and a bath in the scullery contained human remains that had been boiled; in a bedroom was a bloodstained saw; in a trunk, marked with the intials 'EBK', were portions of a woman's body; and in a biscuit tin were the heart and other internal organs.

The atmosphere inside was so dreadful that detectives

The scene outside the Officer's House as Mahon, his head covered, is escorted away.

set up a table in the garden to work on. Police and pathologists found practically the whole body of the victim, a woman probably in an early state of pregnancy with nothing to indicate a natural death.

Emily Kaye was 34 and had worked as a shorthand typist in the City. Long legged, athletic and graceful, she had caught the fancy of Mahon and soon succumbed to his blandishments. They began a love affair and early in 1924 she knew she was pregnant. He had made no secret of the fact that he was married, but he gave her a diamond and sapphire engagement ring and promised to take her to South Africa. On the strength of this she told all her friends what was planned and on 7th April gave up her room at Guildford Street, Bloomsbury.

Police discovered Mahon had bought the knife and saw three days before the alleged quarrel that led to the tragedy, and that Emily Kaye had given most of her £600 savings to her lover – money which had been cashed both before and after her death, the notes endorsed on each occasion with a false name and address. Murder, not an accident, was the line of the police investigation.

Mahon had fleeced the woman who loved him and knew that if the child was born he would be exposed. So he rented the seaside bungalow at The Crumbles under the name Waller and arranged for Miss Kaye to stay with him there. Police never established exactly when he killed her, but it must have been soon after she wrote a last letter to a friend describing her happiness and future travels. She believed she was going to Cape Town to get married.

Before travelling to The Crumbles to keep his fateful appointment with Miss Kaye, Mahon had met Miss Ethel Duncan while walking in Richmond and it is some measure of the charm of the man that on the strength of a casual conversation in the street she had agreed to have dinner with him. They dined at a restaurant in Victoria – possibly on the very day he had killed Emily – and she agreed to spend the Easter holiday with him 'at a friend's bungalow at Eastbourne'.

She arrived on Good Friday and was taken on a motoring tour of Sussex by Mahon, wined and dined and then taken to the bungalow. He was quite normal and in good spirits, she revealed, and she had a fleeting glimpse of the cabin trunk which he told her was used by the friend who owned the property to safeguard valuable books.

Mahon seems to have quickly tired of Miss Duncan. He left her to her own devices in Eastbourne on Saturday while he went to the races at Plumpton (where police believed he changed another of Emily's £100 notes) and sent himself a telegram saying he was required back in the office urgently. He returned to London with Miss Duncan so he could 'answer' the bogus summons.

He then went back to The Crumbles and worked furiously over the next few days at disposing of the body. But for the incriminating contents of the bag at the left luggage cloakroom and the suspicions of his long-suffering wife he might have got away with it. There was nothing to connect Waller of the bungalow with Mahon, the salesman from Kew, and Miss Kaye would not have been reported missing because friends believed she had settled happily in South Africa.

Mahon maintained his smooth style at Lewes Assizes as he battled for his life. Wearing a specially ordered blue suit, his face was tanned (rumour had it, with tobacco juice) and his hands carefully manicured. Only at the end did his composure crack when, under a merciless cross-examination from Sir Henry Curtis-Bennett, he sobbed into a silk handkerchief.

There was an eerie coincidence in the courtroom when a storm broke out as he was desribing the gruesome events at the little house of horrors. Mahon went white despite his tan as he recalled that a storm had raged on the night he put Emily Kaye's head on the fire – her hair had blazed, her eyes had opened in the heat and at that moment a tremendous clap of thunder and lightning played around the room. Mahon had fled from it in terror.

His story that the death had been an accident was dismissed and Mahon went to the gallows on 9th September for 'one of the foulest crimes that has been committed in recent years'. Right until the end the smooth-talking charmer believed he would escape the noose with a successful appeal. When that failed, he fought for life until the last... literally. As the trap was about to fall to launch the condemned man into eternity he desperately threw his feet forward to dodge the void opening beneath him. He failed, and his body crashed back against the scaffold opening as he fell. The routine post mortem on the body of Patrick Mahon showed he had a broken back as well as a broken neck.

The bungalow at The Crumbles held a ghoulish fascination for many years afterwards. It had begun while police were making their sickening discoveries there, with hundreds of the curious packed around the garden fence trying to get a view. They were later able to peer as much as they wanted to, with guided tours of the Officer's House on offer at one shilling and twopence a time and stalls and booths erected in the garden. Violent death and its aftermath became a tourist attraction with holidaymakers flocking to see 'the place where it all happened'.

The building was eventually demolished in 1953 and The Crumbles area has been extensively developed in recent years, but it is still a place heavy in forbidding atmosphere.

3

UNDER THE
CHICKEN RUN

THE MURDER OF ELSIE CAMERON AT
CROWBOROUGH, DECEMBER 1924

John Norman Holmes Thorne was a paragon of virtue in his teenage years, the unlikeliest of candidates for the gallows. At the age of only 15 he was a Sunday school teacher and speaker at Band of Hope meetings, a year later he formed a natural history club for like-minded youngsters and at 17 he founded and ran a troop of 160 Boy Scouts. He was also a stalwart of the Wesley Guild, which involved temperance and social work, organising concerts and open-air gatherings for the faithful.

He was not particularly handsome or dynamic, but he was solid and dependable; the sort of man who marries the girl next door and plods happily through life. While not exactly the girl next door, Elsie Emily Cameron was a close neighbour – her family, like his, lived in the London suburb of Kensal Rise and she had known Thorne from childhood. They shared a common interest in the same Wesleyan church and it came as no surprise when the devout young couple became engaged in 1922 when they were both in their early twenties.

Thorne may have been finding spiritual uplift, but his career prospects had nose-dived after a trade slump forced the closure of the experimental and electrical department of Fiat Motors in London where he was

An unlikely candidate for the gallows . . . John Norman Holmes Thorne.

employed. With the prospect of marriage and responsibility looming, Thorne desperately needed a job and decided to take the drastic step of living off the land. He borrowed £100 from his father, a naval boffin who worked for the Admiralty, and set off for Sussex.

Crowborough in the early 1920s was little more than a village where Edwardian villas branched away along leafy lanes from the original settlement. It prided itself on being something of a resort, where the invigorating breezes of the rolling uplands of north Sussex could work wonders for the health. It had a refreshing climate all its own – draw a line due east of Crowborough Beacon and the first patch of land you hit of corresponding height is deep in Siberia.

Thorne purchased a small field at Luxford Lane, Blackness, then just outside the town, and here he established the aptly named Wesley Poultry Farm. He lived alone in a spartan wooden shack measuring just seven feet by twelve, set amidst the chicken huts and built originally to provide a brooding house. For two years he endured a primitive lifestyle as he struggled to make a living out of the hens. Elsie, working as a typist in London, was a regular weekend visitor, spending the days with Thorne and his poultry collection and the nights in lodgings nearby – with Agnes and Edwin Piper at Pasture Villas and later with Florence and Robert Cosham at Corona in Luxford Lane.

Elsie seems to have been content enough with the arrangement and even managed to spend a six week spell at the farm in the summer of 1923 when she found temporary employment locally as a nursemaid. But there were long days and nights when they were apart and he had only the clucking fowls for company. Perhaps it was inevitable that in the early months of 1924 he should form a friendship with another young lady, the pretty and vivacious Elizabeth Coldicott, a dressmaker who lived with her mother at Springfield in South View Road, Crowborough.

They had met at a dance at Waterloo Hall and continued to meet at later dances, though Thorne was initially perfectly open about their relationship, introducing his intended to his new friend 'Bessie'. Then things became more serious, Thorne found himself falling in love and Bessie responded, becoming a regular visitor to his hut where he confided his doubts about Elsie as a future wife and suggested that he should break off the engagement and marry Bessie instead.

Elsie continued to spend her weekends in Sussex, but she must have sensed by his change in attitude that something was wrong and started to suffer bouts of deep depression. Finally he plucked up the courage to be honest and in an exchange of letters confessed that he felt 'between two fires', having to choose between his childhood sweetheart and the exciting new woman in his life.

The news did not go down well. Elsie, miserable and desperate that November, decided to apply maximum emotional pressure to get her man; she sent him a letter saying she was pregnant and the child was his, adding, 'You have absolutely broken my heart, I never thought you were capable of such deception. You are engaged to me and I have first claim on you. Well, Norman, I expect you to marry me, and finish with the other girl as soon as possible. My baby must have a name.'

She arrived, unexpected, at Wesley Poultry Farm on Sunday, 30th November, in a further bid to persuade Thorne, but the meeting must have been decidedly frosty on his part for he chivvied her back to Groombridge and the London train so he could meet Bessie that same evening.

Five days later she tried again with a little more hope in her heart, perhaps, for she had been told by a fortune teller that she would marry in December. It was Friday,

5th December, and she had taken considerable trouble to improve her appearance by getting a brand new hairstyle that morning, putting on a new silk jumper and a smart pair of shoes. Without telling her father where she was going, she caught the 2 pm train from Kensal Rise, heading for Sussex with her belongings neatly packed in a suitcase.

She arrived at the farm late that afternoon, hoping for a romantic reconciliation with the man she loved. Instead the decent, God-fearing poultry farmer became a killer.

Elsie stood in the way of all his hopes of future happiness. Their engagement had been a mistake and now her pregnancy was about to trap him into a loveless, empty marriage. Exactly what went on in the tiny shack between the hours of 5.15 pm and 9.30 pm will never be known because Thorne never admitted to an attack, but Elsie was pounded with a blunt instrument, possibly a wooden stake or one of several indian clubs kept in the hut. No bones were broken, but she suffered serious bruising to her legs and arms and two violent blows to either side of her face which led rapidly to her death.

Thorne then hurried off to Crowborough station where he had an appointment at 9.30 pm to meet Bessie Coldicott and her mother who were returning from a day trip to Brighton. He walked them both home and kissed his new love goodnight at the gate. Then he returned to his farm and a hideous nightshift.

Working by the glow of the fire in the hut. Thorne used a hacksaw to carve Elsie's body into four sections. Then he began to dig. The severed legs were tied together with string, wrapped in sacking and buried nearly two feet deep in the Wealden clay of the chicken run, as were the arms and torso. The head was bound with sacking, too, then stuffed into a tin box and buried close to the rest of the poor girl.

Her suitcase filled a hole he made in a potato patch near

the farm gate, and some of her valuables, including a gold wristwatch, he stuffed into an old Oxo tin and hid in the tool shed. He must have had time to snatch a little sleep and spruce himself up before dashing off to visit Bessie. He took her to Crowborough's small picture house and behaved perfectly normally.

Elsie's father only became anxious five days after her disappearance when he sent a telegram to Thorne, assuming that Crowborough had been her destination, but received an immediate reply that she had not been seen at the farm. Puzzled and worried, Mr Cameron went to the police, who centred their search on London where she had last been seen.

But police in Sussex had also begun to make enquiries, with the full co-operation of the missing girl's boyfriend. Thorne allowed them to make a search of his property and supplied a snapshot of Elsie which appeared in the *Police Gazette*. He told Inspector George Edwards of Crowborough and Superintendent Isaac Budgen of Uckfield that he had last seen her on 30th November. She had been due to visit him again on Saturday, 6th December, he said, but had not turned up at Groombridge railway station when he went to meet her.

Locally, Thorne speculated wildly that she might have committed suicide by jumping into the Thames, that she had collapsed by some country wayside and been taken by gipsies, even that 'the Mormons might have got hold of her'. These tales did not carry much weight with Jarvis Brook nursery workers George Adams and Albert Sands, who both recalled seeing a young woman with a suitcase walking along Luxford Road at Blackness towards Thorne's farm soon after 5 pm on 5th December. The police asked more questions but were met with another flat denial, and obviously tended to believe his version of events.

Thorne was able to spend Christmas with his new love

and on New Year's Day wrote Bessie a tender letter. '...
I believe meeting you is the richest blessing I have ever
had and however some may talk and laugh at love, it is
the sweetest and dearest thing I have found...' But time
was running out. He thought he had got away with
murder, and the bliss he believed lay ahead as they went
through the threshold of 1925 was destined to be
short-lived.

It was on 10th January that a third witness came
forward to say she had seen Elsie. Mrs Annie Price, of
Blackness Cottages, was something of a recluse and kept
herself to herself. She had been unaware of any missing
woman until a chance glance through the local paper. Mrs
Price told the police she had been out walking and
spotted a young woman going through the gate of the
Wesley Poultry Farm.

The Chief Constable of Sussex responded quickly to
this new and significant development by asking for help
from Scotland Yard. Chief Inspector John Gillan and
Detective Sergeant Ambrose Askew hastened down to
Crowborough and a dramatic confrontation with
Thorne.

He stuck to his guns, saying Elsie Cameron had not
been near the premises on 5th December. In a lengthy
interview at Crowborough police station he even said he
had no objection to police digging on his land. They
called his bluff and early on the morning of 15th January
PC John Philpott went to work with a spade in the potato
plot. In no time he struck something hard, and unearthed
the suitcase containing Elsie's easily identified clothing.
Gillan told Thorne, 'You will now be detained and
charged with causing the death of Elsie Cameron.' There
was no response.

The chicken farmer stayed silent for the rest of the day
while in custody, but finally that evening decided to
make a new statement. It had been a nightmare series of

events, he said. Elsie had turned up on that fateful Friday, declaring she was pregnant and demanding marriage. The situation was discussed over tea, said Thorne, and at 9.30 pm he had left her alone in the hut while he went to meet Bessie. When he returned at 11.30 pm he was horrified to find Elsie hanging from a roof beam on the end of his washing line. He had panicked and, fearing he would be blamed for her suicide, decided to dispose of her body. He told police exactly where to dig to find the various parts.

It was by now late in the evening, but the police were not prepared to wait for daylight. They began digging in the first chicken pen inside the farm gate and there, just below the surface, recovered two heavy parcels and one large tin box. Thorne was charged with the murder at 2.15 pm the following day.

The great legal and medical minds of the day drew up battle lines for the trial of John Norman Thorne at Lewes Assizes on 4th March. The chief weapon of the prosecution was Sir Bernard Spilsbury, the most experienced criminal pathologist of his generation, who had examined the remains soon after they had been recovered. He found no cuts or abrasions to the body, and no broken bones, but he did identify eight significant bruises, 'all inflicted shortly before death and in the case of two of them they were immediately followed by death.' He came to the conclusion that death was caused by shock due to the injuries on the head and limbs.

The eloquent King's Counsel appointed to defend Thorne was Mr J.D. Cassels who had (unsuccessfully) fought for the life of Crumbles murderer Patrick Mahon only the previous year. He arranged for Elsie's body to be exhumed from Willesden cemetery, where she had been buried on 26th January, so an independent examination for the defence could be made by eminent pathologist Dr

Robert Bronte, former crown analyst to the Irish Government.

He argued that some bruises may have been caused before death and some after, and that blows violent enough to have been fatal would have broken the skin. He backed Thorne's suicide story by revealing that on examining the dead woman's neck he had found abnormal creases, which could have been made by a thin rope or cord. He also found broken blood vessels at the neck, consistent with hanging.

The accused told the court that he had cut Elsie down from the beam but she was dead. 'I realised the precarious position I was in. I decided I must do all I could to hide every trace of the suicide. I pulled off her clothes and most of them I placed on the fire, I divided the body and placed the remains in the sacks.'

The formidable Spilsbury said he found 'no indications of asphyxia whatever. In my examination I found no natural disease to account for death nor any indication external or internal that death had been caused by hanging.'

The drastic variance in the evidence presented a dilemma to the jury, but they got a little help thanks to an experiment carried out by the police. They suspended a hundredweight sack from a cord thrown over the beam in Thorne's shack and found it cut into the soft wood, leaving an indentation. There was no such mark at the point on the beam where Thorne said he found Elsie's body dangling.

The jury took less than 30 minutes to find Thorne guilty of murder. Despite the conflicting medical evidence, perhaps they thought the natural reaction of a man who finds a woman dead in his home would be to get help, not cut up her body and conceal it. Perhaps, too, they were swayed by the reputation of Spilsbury, even though the great man's evidence had been challenged by Bronte and no fewer than seven other doctors in court – one of them Dr Hugh Miller Gault, pathologist at Brighton's Royal Sussex County Hospital.

Thorne certainly thought so. In his last interview with his father after the Home Secretary had refused a reprieve, he said, 'Never mind, Dad, don't worry, I'm a martyr to Spilsburyism.' He was hanged at Wandsworth on 22nd April 1925. It would have been Elsie's 27th birthday.

Long after the execution the case continued to attract public attention, with a big question mark over whether justice had truly been done. The creator of Sherlock Holmes, Sir Arthur Conan Doyle, who lived at Windlesham Manor, Crowborough, and had taken a close interest in the affair, was one of many people who doubted if the case had been satisfactorily proved. And the staid *Law Journal* commented that the execution would leave a feeling of profound disquiet.

There was one thing, though, that all the medical men at the trial did agree upon: Elsie Cameron was not, and never had been, pregnant.

4

LEFT LUGGAGE

THE DEATH OF VIOLET KAYE AT BRIGHTON, MAY 1934

Nobody can have been more surprised than Tony Mancini in June 1934 when it was announced that parts of a dead woman had been discovered in the left luggage office at Brighton station. He must have reflected that it was a rare old summer on the south coast.

For Mancini, a former boxer turned Soho tough who had sought dubious 'retirement' in 'London-by-the-Sea', had been living with a grisly secret of his own for several weeks, literally. Beside his bed he kept a large cabin trunk. His landlady thought it contained all his worldly possessions. In fact it harboured the rotting corpse of his lover, Violet Kaye.

He had bought the trunk for 7s 6d from a stall in Brighton market, put the dead body inside it and slept with it beside him for at least six weeks. How he managed to sleep was never explained. Other tenants of the flats in Kemp Street often complained about the smell emerging from the rooms of their tough neighbour as June 1934 progressed into a hot July. His landlady pointed out in dismay that liquids were oozing from the trunk. Mancini responded by wiping out the seeping body fluids and putting down disinfectant.

He was 25 when Violet had persuaded him to leave London, where he supplied the muscle for the ruthless racketeers in Soho, and join her in Brighton. The nature

28

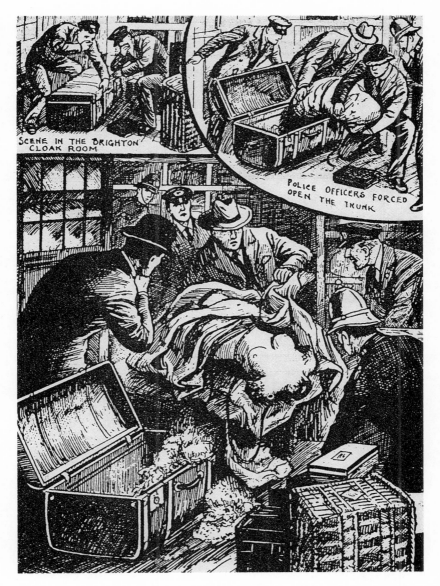

The discovery of the 'other' victim – Mancini was also interviewed for this crime.

of his business meant Mancini had made enemies – he had recently been severely beaten in a brawl at a nightclub where he worked as a bouncer – and an excuse to get away from the capital for a while probably appealed to him. Besides, Violet was still attractive at 41 and he found the attentions of an older woman flattering. Violet was a tragic figure. She had forsaken a promising career on the stage as a singer and dancer for a life of prostitution. With a failed marriage behind her, she often sought solace in the bottle or in occasional doses of morphine.

The unlikely couple led a seedy life together in a basement at 44 Park Crescent, with Mancini largely playing the role of 'minder' while Violet entertained her clients. A genuine affection certainly existed for a time – he would help her count the takings at the end of an evening's work and they often strolled together along the seafront – but the relationship was barely a year old when it ended abruptly in May 1934.

Mancini told friends that Violet had left Brighton to take up a good job in Paris. Her sister even received a telegram to that effect, saying 'Going abroad. Good job. Sail Sunday. Will write – V'. Alone, he humped the cabin trunk containing 'all his worldly possessions' to a new address at 55 Kemp Street, another basement room, in the heart of Brighton's North Lanes and close to the busy main-line station.

He appears to have stayed there happily, apart from the occasional olfactory complaints of fellow tenants, until Sunday 17th June, when the Brighton police shattered the seaside summer with their sensational discovery of a dismembered female in a trunk at the left luggage office. They had been alerted by station staff alarmed by the nauseous smell.

Only the torso remained, the head, arms and legs having been hacked off the naked body. The trunk had

30

been deposited on the evening of 6th June by an unidentified customer. Police found the only possible clue to the woman's identity was some recent writing in blue pencil on a sheet of brown paper inside the trunk. All that could be read were the letters '... FORD', the preceding part of the word having been completely obscured by dried blood. Pathologist Sir Bernard Spilsbury established that the woman was about 25, and four to five months pregnant. She had been dismembered by an unskilled hand shortly after death.

The riddle occupied Britain's police forces for the next twelve months and must have left Mancini bemused.

The severed legs and feet of the left luggage torso were discovered three days later, packed inside a small suitcase at King's Cross railway station in London. Again, staff had picked it out as suspicious because of the offensive odour. The remains were wrapped in copies of the *Daily Mail* dated 31st May and 2nd June 1934. The new finds fitted the torso exactly. Railway employees up and down the country were now engaged in the search for the missing head and arms, and the police launched a massive investigation without making any real progress.

The name of Violet Kaye was put forward as a missing person by a friend who obviously did not trust Mancini, but she was dismissed as the trunk victim – Violet was in her forties, had given birth before and was a well-known prostitute. However, Mancini was called in for interview by the police. Perfectly composed, he said Violet had left him to live with another man. He firmly denied the suggestion that he had given away items of female clothing to other women in Brighton. Police kept a watch on the swarthy bruiser and he realised it, because he caught an early train from Preston Park and headed back to the anonymity of London. He was in such a hurry to get away that he left his precious trunk behind.

A painter and decorator had been employed by the

owners of the Kemp Street boarding house to give the place a facelift. He noticed an awful smell coming from a cupboard in one of the unoccupied rooms. Knowing of the trunk murder case and the search for the rest of the body, he went straight to the police station.

Detectives descended on 55 Kemp Street convinced they would discover the head and arms of the murder victim. Instead, they encountered a completely separate mystery. Grotesquely stuffed inside a putrid cabin trunk was a complete female body. The identity was swiftly established: Violet Kaye, dead for at least eight weeks and rapidly decomposing.

The remains of one body in a trunk was sensational. Two bodies in two different trunks gave the case worldwide notoriety.

Mancini, as the last occupier of the flat, was tracked down within two days, 'a nervous and hesitant' figure found walking the London to Maidstone road near Sidcup in the early hours of 17th July.

He firmly denied killing Violet, but admitted keeping her body hidden. He said he had found her body at the flat they shared in Park Crescent, her knees almost touching her chin, clutching at a handful of sheets. She had a handkerchief around her neck and there was blood everywhere. He assumed she was the victim of one of her more violent customers, of whom he knew there were several. He had not alerted the police, he said, because he doubted he would get a fair hearing because of his criminal record. He had simply bought a trunk at the market and concealed the body.

The evidence against Mancini was overwhelming. Pathologist Spilsbury deduced that Violet had died following a depressed fracture of the skull, inflicted with considerable force by a blunt instrument, possibly the head of a hammer. Detectives found a collection of Mancini's clothes splashed with blood and a hammer was recovered from the basement at Park Crescent which was almost certainly the murder weapon. Mancini himself admitted that he had forged the telegram to Violet's sister. Fifty witnesses at Brighton magistrates court attested to his violent nature and his threats towards Violet, and he looked doomed when the trial began at Lewes Assizes on 10th December. But he had a brilliant advocate in Norman Birkett who, against all the odds, demolished the prosecution case piece by piece.

He described his client as 'idle, worthless, a man without morals or principles', but not a murderer. Violet, he argued, under the influence of drugs or alcohol, might well have fallen down the steps of the basement flat to her death. He managed to cast sufficient doubt into the minds of the jury that at the end of two and half hours they emerged with a verdict of not guilty. An amazed Mancini walked out of court a free man.

The police were furious, of course. The Scotland Yard team had been confident that they had solved one of the two cases attracting worldwide attention. Now the hundreds of hours that had gone into the two murder investigations had left them with nothing but one unidentified body and one unsuccessful prosecution.

More than 40 years later, at the age of 69, Mancini was persuaded to give an interview at his home in the north of England to a *News of the World* journalist in which he confessed to killing Violet. Two years later he repeated this in another newspaper story, saying he had killed her during a violent row. He had punched her on the chin, he said, and then, in a blind rage, banged her head on the fender at Park Crescent.

As a result a senior Sussex detective was given the task of reopening the infamous Brighton trunk murders file in 1976. But time had made murky the bright trail of the past.

The Director of Public Prosecutions stated that

independent corroboration of Mancini's claim was essential and because of the years elapsed between 1934 and 1976 this would not now be available. In a letter to the Chief Constable of Sussex he finally brought the saga to an end: 'My opinion is that there is insufficient evidence available or likely to become available to prosecute Mancini for perjury.'

It is hard not to sympathise with the police. By an uncanny coincidence two killers of women left bodies in not dissimilar trunks in the same neighbourhood of the same town within three weeks of each other. Confusion was understandable and possibly clouded the minds of the jury when they considered Mancini's case.

The fate and identity of Violet Kaye was established, if not her killer. But who was 'victim number one', the well-nourished, pregnant young woman found severally at Brighton and King's Cross?

The word 'FORD' in blue pencil eventually took police to a confectionery factory in Finsbury Park, London, where a secretary identified her own writing. The *Daily Express* offered a £500 reward for information and a professional medium presented police with 'clues'. None of which has ever led to the identity of the unfortunate in the left luggage office.

5

THE MURDER
IN THE PARK

THE MURDER OF JOAN WOODHOUSE AT ARUNDEL, JULY 1948

The reason why Joan Woodhouse made her fatal journey to Sussex in the summer of 1948 is still as much a mystery today as the identity of her murderer. She should have been 200 miles away from the secluded beauty spot where she was raped and strangled.

Her father was a widower who lived in Barnsley, Yorkshire, and studious Joan had arranged to spend the August Bank Holiday weekend with him. As her body lay undiscovered and decomposing during the days that followed the brutal killing, he was to send a plaintive telegram to her London hostel 'Are you OK? If not come home. Auntie is worried.'

Numerous individuals have 'confessed' to the murder down the years, from an unemployed piano tuner and a British Rail cleaner to a former Navy dentist and a Yugoslavian refugee described as a 'sexual neurotic'. All have been investigated and eliminated as attention-seeking cranks by the Sussex police, leaving a glaring unsolved crime on the files.

Joan was a respectable and serious-minded young woman of 27 with strong religious beliefs who worked as a librarian in central London. In 1947 she had fallen in love with a fellow librarian called Edward Roberts, and the pair looked destined to marry. However, early in 1948 their romance ended in a quarrel and Joan was devastated.

She suffered a nervous breakdown and came close to suicide, but was nursed back to health by two devoted aunts in Bridlington, on the Yorkshire coast. Her doctor was so concerned about her mental state when she returned to work that he insisted she should not live alone, so she found accommodation at the YWCA hostel at Blackheath, where she soon made several good friends.

She told her room-mate she was going north to see her father when she set out at 8.30 am on Saturday, 31st July, wearing an eye-catching blue paisley dress with yellow and pink stripes and carrying a handbag and suitcase. For some inexplicable reason she caught a train going in completely the opposite direction – to the south coast. One theory is that she was still feeling depressed and wanted to return to a place that held happy childhood memories for her. Her aunts had shared a house in Worthing before their move to Bridlington and Joan had been a regular visitor as a youngster. She had particularly enjoyed summer picnics in Arundel Park, the Duke of Norfolk's rolling acres of hills and woods where her body was found ten days later.

It was to Worthing that Joan came first on that sunny Saturday, depositing her suitcase containing clothing, letters and £7 in cash at the Left Luggage Office of Worthing Central station at around noon. She must then have boarded a bus for picturesque Arundel some nine miles away. At 2 pm she bought a bottle of barley water at the chemist's shop in the High Street, and was seen alone in The Square at about 2.30 pm.

She then made her way under the rugged walls of Arundel Castle into the park, walking in her light sandals beside Swanbourne Lake, busy and noisy that day with boaters. Joan sought seclusion deeper in the park and wandered for nearly a mile along the footpath before climbing up a steep hill and into the lush green of Box Copse.

She found a clearing among the trees and appears to have settled down to sunbathe away from prying eyes, spreading her raincoat on the ground and folding a lightweight coat to make a pillow for her head. She slipped off the multicoloured dress and laid it, neatly folded, beside her with her brown sling bag, and artificial pearl necklace, a pair of sunglasses and the bottle of barley water.

What happened in the minutes that followed will probably never be known. Joan, in her state of partial undress, must have been taken by surprise by her assailant. Startled, she jumped to her feet and attempted to escape. She did not get far. Her body was found only twelve yards from her pile of possessions. She had been subjected to a violent sexual assault and strangled. Then the killer had fled, making no attempt at concealment or robbery.

Many walkers must have passed near the scene that Bank Holiday weekend and in the days that followed, but none entered Box Copse and it was not until the afternoon of Tuesday 10th August that Joan's rapidly decomposing corpse was found. The horrifying discovery was made by an Arundel house painter by the name of Thomas Stillwell who little knew, as he breathlessly alerted the police in Arundel at 5.20 pm, that his own private nightmare was about to begin.

The sleepy little town was suddenly thrust into the national spotlight as a full murder investigation was launched by Scotland Yard. But they made a mistake right at the start – and spent precious weeks looking for a man who did not exist. Police were convinced Joan was conducting a secret affair and had gone to Worthing with a man friend or had met a man in the town, and that the

Joan Woodhouse, right, out with a group of friends.

couple had gone to Arundel Park and she had been partly responsible for any sexual act that took place.

So it was at Worthing that they launched a massive door-to-door hunt. Every hotel and boarding house was shown a photograph of the victim and asked if she had booked accommodation for herself and a man on the night of the 31st July. They traced every single male that had stayed in the town that weekend and then turned their attention to Arundel, where the process was repeated.

Detective Chief Inspector Fred Narborough was nothing less than thorough. He insisted on tracing every holidaymaker who had been in Worthing and Arundel on 31st July and had the local police visit them in their homes. British Rail staff at Victoria, Worthing and Arundel were all interviewed, as were coach drivers and conductors operating between London and the coast. Every male over 15 years of age in Arundel was closely questioned.

The enquiry spread further afield to include students and male colleagues from Joan's college days and her ex-fiancé had to satisfy police about his movements. By now it was almost October and Scotland Yard had to face the fact that they had been wasting time and energy; Joan Woodhouse did not have a man in her life, and she was certainly not a woman of 'easy virtue'.

Narborough was forced to admit later, 'I became satisfied that Miss Woodhouse was of exemplary character, went to the park alone, climbed to this lovely secluded spot where she removed her frock, either to sunbathe or because she was hot, and that she was there gravely indecently assaulted and murdered by a man who was a complete stranger to her . . . her bestial assailant leaving her to her fate, neither knowing or caring what it would be.'

The hunt switched from shadowy boyfriend to

Peeping Tom, a man who had spotted the scantily-clad young woman among the trees and totally lost control.

Narborough began to focus his attention on the young man who had discovered the body, 24 year old Thomas Philip George Stillwell. He had been helpful with the investigation and had given a routine statement on 11th August about finding the victim. There had then been no reason to doubt his story, but later interviews with witnesses indicated that Stillwell had been in the park on the day of the murder – and more than one person asserted that he had been talking to a young woman who closely resembled Joan Woodhouse.

During further interviews, the house painter admitted he had said 'Good morning, lovely day' to a girl walking away from Box Copse. She 'seemed to be very nervous' and hurried off. When shown a picture of the victim he told police he could not be sure if it was the same person he had greeted. Besides, it had been morning – and Joan did not reach the park until well into the afternoon.

A month went by before Stillwell was subjected to an intensive examination by detectives. This time he was to produce a more detailed, and controversial, statement about his movements on 31st July. He admitted that he could have seen the girl in the park during the early afternoon, though he could not be precise about the time. He had been in Arundel at 3.30 pm to meet a girl called Gwen off the bus, but when she failed to turn up he had travelled alone to the seaside town of Littlehampton. Here he bought a shirt, went to the cinema and returned to Arundel in time for a session of darts at The Newburgh public house which ended at around 11.25 pm when he went home.

The interrogation continued all night. Stillwell simply repeated his original story, though the morning walk had switched to afternoon, and told police, 'Although all the facts about this case seem to point to me, I am perfectly innocent and have no connection with the death of Miss Woodhouse. This girl I saw on the pathway, I do not know who she was but I do not believe it was Joan Woodhouse.'

There was insufficient evidence for the police to proceed further, and with the inquest's verdict of 'murder by some person or persons unknown', Scotland Yard beat a retreat.

Joan's family would not let the matter rest. Stunned by her death and the failure of the authorities to find the culprit, her two aunts employed a Bridlington private detective, Thomas Percy Jacks, who doggedly fought on their behalf – and pulled off a legal coup.

He met with local resistance when he sought to reopen the case, not least because a reward of £500 had been offered in an advertisement in the *News of the World* for new information. Police believed such a financial inducement would simply result in false leads and a waste of their time. Undeterred, Jacks pressed on. He talked at length with the known witnesses and compiled a completely new dossier on the crime, which the national press seized with eagerness. As the speculation grew, the tongues wagged and a furious Stillwell hit back. He held a secret meeting with a journalist in a hotel room which resulted in headlines in the *Sunday Pictorial* condemning the 'local gossip' which was ruining the life of a young man and his new fiancée.

The persistence of Jacks paid off. Two years after the discovery of Joan Woodhouse's body, the private detective and the victim's father put in motion the procedure to obtain a warrant for an arrest. Remarkably, it was the first such application since 1865. Magistrates heard testimony from five witnesses in a private session at Littlehampton on 30th August, 1950, and it led them to sanction the arrest of Thomas Stillwell on a charge of murder.

Protesting his innocence, he was taken to Brixton prison to await trial while a third investigation into the murder was launched. But the evidence was old and the memories hazy when Arundel Magistrates sat for four days in early September to hear the evidence of 35 witnesses. Even the prosecuting counsel had to lamely admit that the evidence against the defendant was 'wholly circumstantial'. The discovery of a dart near the murder scene had little impact. Stillwell freely admitted it was his, and had even reported its loss to the police.

Defence solicitor Mr V.H.O. Jackson, in his final address on behalf of his client, stressed the discrepancies over dates, times and sightings. He told the bench, 'I say therefore that some man got in touch with this woman and got into violent sexual intercourse with her. But who that man was we do not know. This case has been going on for two years and now has come this very great strain upon the accused. He has been held in custody since the end of August and I ask you to remember that if he is committed he will have to wait months for trial. These have been weeks of horror for him and I ask you to say that there is no evidence at all that he was the man who murdered this woman on July 31st, 1948, and that there is no case to answer.'

It took the magistrates two hours to reach their unanimous decision, that there was not enough evidence to justify sending the case for trial and therefore Stillwell should be discharged.

It was not the complete vindication he might have wanted...but if the case had gone to a higher court, Stillwell would have been fighting for his very life. He went on painting the houses of Arundel until his retirement, and always strongly denied any involvement in the crime.

6

THE ACID
BATH KILLER

THE MURDER OF OLIVE DURAND-DEACON AT
CRAWLEY, FEBRUARY 1949

Dapper little Mr Haigh piled horror upon horror when he tried to escape the gallows. The British public were shocked enough over their breakfast tables to read about murder victims being dissolved in acid. To be informed that the killer also drank the blood of his victims was the wrong side of enough.

Fleet Street loved it, of course, and John George Haigh became The Vampire of screaming headlines. He candidly told police that the motive for his years of carnage (the Scotland Yard tally was six murders; Haigh himself said it might have been a dozen or more) had been his desire to drink blood. He even described how he had made an incision in the neck to obtain a cupful.

The lawyers and psychiatrists drawn into the notorious case were convinced it was an invention so he could claim insanity and avoid the noose. On his arrest he had asked, almost conversationally, what the chances were of anyone being released from Broadmoor. Far more chilling were the words, 'If I told you the truth you wouldn't believe me. It sounds too fantastic for belief.'

He was confessing to the murder of Mrs Olive Durand-Deacon at his shabby (and bogus) engineering works in Crawley in the spring of 1949. Haigh boasted, 'Mrs

Durand-Deacon no longer exists. She has completely disappeared and no trace of her can ever be found... I have destroyed her with acid.' But he was wrong. Painstaking forensic work played a key part in the ultimate conviction of a man so dazzlingly charming when he wanted to be that people who professed to know him well could not accept that the same person was capable of such depraved crimes.

Portly 69 year old Mrs Durand-Deacon was the last of his victims, selected, as usual, for financial gain. He had met the wealthy widow while they were both residents of the Onslow Court Hotel in London, and it was she who suggested the manufacture of a new range of plastic fingernails. She had the money to invest and he (she believed) had the factory and engineering expertise.

Haigh made careful preparations at his premises in Leopold Road, Crawley, and then met Mrs Durand-Deacon outside the Army and Navy Stores in Victoria on the afternoon of Friday, 18th February. They set off for Sussex in his maroon Alvis to supposedly explore the potential of their little scheme. Her trust in the 39 year old businessman and fellow hotel resident was obviously total.

She probably had little time for second thoughts when she saw the dingy reality of 'the factory', little more than a storehouse but with three sparkling new ten-gallon carboys of concentrated sulphuric acid. Haigh shot her in the back of the head with his .38 Enfield pistol, removed her Persian lamb coat and jewellery and dumped her fully clothed body into a 40-gallon tank.

The man who had first experimented with the effects of acid on field mice then went for an egg on toast and a cup of tea at the café across the road. He returned to don his rubber protective clothing and gas mask and pump concentrated sulphuric acid into the tank, remembering that after 20 to 30 minutes it would become

Mrs Olive Durand-Deacon – the last of Haigh's victims.

too hot to touch. Finally he left for dinner at The George Hotel before returning to the London hotel.

Haigh was back in Crawley three days later to complete the job. He examined the tank and its contents and pumped in more acid. Judging decomposition complete the following day, he pumped off the contents into the overgrown area outside the storehouse known as Giles Yard.

His arrest and confession came a week later. A friend of the victim was worried by her disappearance after her rendezvous with Haigh, and Haigh himself volunteered to accompany her to the police because he 'thought he might help'.

Police suspicions grew when they discovered that the man so anxious to give them a helping hand in their investigation had a criminal record for fraud and theft. They invited him to Chelsea police station after establishing that Mrs Durand-Deacon's jewellery had been sold to a shop in Horsham for £100 and that a cleaner's receipt for her Persian lamb coat, dated the day after her disappearance, had been found at Haigh's storeroom, together with the acid, the grotesque rubber wear, revolver and ammunition.

He confessed to the killing and then asked his question about Broadmoor, the prison for the criminally insane. He also seemed to be under the misapprehension that because there was no body he could not be tried for murder.

The rough ground outside the storeroom was covered with pebbles, but there was one in particular that pathologist Professor Keith Simpson was looking for in Giles Yard, taking into account the nature of the crime and the age and habits of the missing widow. He found what he was looking for almost immediately – a 'pebble' about the size of a cherry with polished facets. Laboratory tests proved it to be a human gallstone.

That was not all. Embedded in a thick, charred, greasy substance were several pieces of eroded bone, the greater part of a left foot, and inside the green painted steel drum in which the body had been digested the professor saw a hairpin stuck in the grease at the bottom.

An area of yellowish sludge measuring six feet by four feet, and three to four inches deep, was dug up and packed into boxes for patient sifting at the laboratory. Altogether some 475 lb of grease and earth were transported to Scotland Yard and from this the scientists were able to reconstruct the body of an elderly, slightly arthritic woman with gallstones, who had false teeth of an unusual kind, a left foot that fitted a particular shoe, and who had been carrying a red plastic handbag with a lipstick container in it. From the amount of body fat they discovered, they knew she was stoutly built.

It was for the murder of Mrs Durand-Deacon that Haigh was tried in a celebrated trial at Lewes Assize Court. But before her, the little man readily admitted, there had been William 'Mac' McSwan and his parents Donald and Amy, a family that had befriended Haigh. All were murdered and dissolved in 1944 and flushed into the London sewers.

Then there were wealthy members of London society Dr Archie Henderson and his attractive wife Rose, into whose circle Haigh had ingratiated himself. He became a regular guest at house parties and played the baby grand to help the entertainment go with a swing. They died on 14th February 1948, lured separately to Leopold Road from The Metropole Hotel, Brighton, where they were staying, shot and left to disintegrate in the acid-filled oil drums. All the murders had been for money and possessions of the victims and it is extraordinary that Haigh was able to bluff his way past even the most astute of lawyers and businessmen.

His defence counsel, David Maxwell Fyfe, told the

packed, shocked courtroom at Lewes that Haigh was guilty but insane and asked the jury to return that verdict. The Attorney General, Sir Hartley Shawcross, said there was a perfectly rational explanation for what had happened – greed.

The much-hyped trial lasted only two days and the jury took only 18 minutes to decide that Haigh was both guilty and sane. He showed no emotion at the verdict and went to the gallows at Wandsworth prison on 10th August 1949, shortly after his fortieth birthday and after donating his green hopsack suit to Madame Tussaud's waxwork museum in London where they were constructing a wax figure of him for the Chamber of Horrors.

Genial to the end . . . John George Haigh raises a smile after a court appearance.

The man who thought he had got the bizarre nature of his killing down to a fine art had proved too impatient with his last victim. The case aroused considerable medical and scientific interest and there were a number of experiments which indicated that about a month of immersion would have destroyed all the exhibits that sent him to the rope. Except the gallstone.

But Haigh had found international notoriety. He wrote to his parents from prison, 'It isn't everybody who can create more sensation than a film star. Only Princess Margaret or Mr Churchill could command such interest.'

7

PORTRAIT OF DEATH

THE MURDER OF MARGARET SPEVICK AT HOVE, FEBRUARY 1954

The murder of a child will always arouse public anger. William Sanchez de Pina Hepper must have felt acutely that the mob was baying for his blood when he stood in the dock at Lewes Assizes in July 1954. He was on trial for the brutal rape and killing of eleven year old Margaret Rose Spevick at his flat in Hove.

Little Margaret, affectionately known as Margot, was great friends at school in Victoria, London, with Pearl Hepper. Their families lived in the same area of Chelsea and Pearl's parents also had a small seaside flat in Hove, so it seemed natural when Mrs Spevick received a letter on 17th January 1954, inviting Margaret down to the coast to convalesce after an unfortunate fall had resulted in a simple fracture of her arm.

Besides, 62 year old William Hepper had a reputation as a local artist and was keen to paint the portrait of his daughter's friend. He assured Margaret's mother that all the child's medical requirements would be attended to, and there were fond farewells when Hepper collected her on 3rd February for her trip to the coast.

Mrs Spevick had arranged to travel down herself to visit her daughter later in the week. She expected to be met at Brighton station, but on the appointed day there was no sign of Hepper and, after waiting in vain for two hours, she was obliged to take the London train home.

She managed to find the Hove address and sped south again with vague misgivings. She got no reply when she called at the flat and waited outside with such growing distress that the tenant of another flat, Mrs Holly, took pity on her. Together they enlisted the help of the caretaker to get into Hepper's home.

It was Mrs Holly who found Margaret. She saw a child's foot sticking out of the end of the bed and pulled back the blankets to see the little girl lying naked and dead. Next to the bed was the macabre presence of an artist's easel. Propped on it was an unfinished portrait of Margaret Spevick.

Police put together the victim's last days. Margaret had been seen with Hepper by Mrs Holly two days earlier, and that evening a Major Davey had visited Hepper and talked with the girl. Hepper had spoken of going to Gibraltar. A massive search was launched for him. The newspapers carried his portrait and it was displayed on cinema screens. The police also broadcast the wanted man's description for only the second time in the history of the BBC.

Hepper's hiding place was discovered in the Spanish border town of Irun, from where he sent friends in Gibraltar a postcard. He was detained in prison at San Sebastian while his extradition was arranged and then escorted back to Britain by Detective Inspector Reginald Bidgood of Hove CID.

In response to a request by DI Bidgood to explain Margaret's death, Hepper had said, 'That is impossible. I cannot remember since I lost my memory in Brighton until I come round a few days ago.'

This was to be the basis of his defence before Mr Justice Jones at Lewes Assizes and his counsel, Mr Derek Curtis-Bennett, said Hepper was the victim of a mental disorder known as paranoia. The accused man's father had, in fact, died confined in a Madrid asylum.

51

Hepper told the court that on arriving in Hove with Margaret on 3rd February, he found a letter stating that his brother was dangerously ill in Spain and decided to rush to his sick bed. He and the child were both upset that their holiday was to be cut short, but he gave her a spare key and a ten shilling note for her fare home if she left while he was abroad.

On the following evening, he maintained, he suffered a severe asthma attack and went walking on the beach to take in the sea air. When he returned he took some tablets with a glass of brandy and fell into a deep sleep. Hepper's bizarre recollection of that night as he told it in the witness box was as follows:

Hepper: I had a terrible dream; I saw my wife coming into the room with a man I know very well and I got up from the chair and followed them to the corridor outside my room.

Mr Justice Jones: Whom did you follow?

Hepper: The man. My wife stayed in the room. The man disappeared in the dark. I went back into the room and had a discussion with my wife and accused her of infidelity.

Mr Justice Jones: This is still a dream, isn't it?

Hepper: Yes, my lord...then we had like a fighting, and she fell on the floor, suffering from pain because we had a fight. Later, I woke up and found nobody in the room. It was about six o'clock in the morning. I took the first train to Victoria, where I buy a ticket as far as Paris. I don't remember reaching Spain.

Hepper's quite irrational accusations of his wife's infidelity were not entirely new. While incarcerated at San Sebastian two months previously he had written an eccentric letter to the Spanish Ambassador in London, stating that his wife had said she hated him and was in love with another man. Hepper's London doctor, too, had received a similar letter, which Dr Hugh

Gainsborough considered a false and scurrilous slight on a devoted and long-suffering wife.

There was drama in court the following day when the accused collapsed. A doctor rushed to attend him but could find nothing wrong, saying, 'I cannot find any physical cause for his collapse. His pulse is normal. He is just lying down and will not speak to me, and will not co-operate to the extent of taking smelling salts.'

Was it a genuine psychotic attack, or was Hepper desperately trying to play crazy and bolster his defence?

A succession of doctors and psychiatrists argued for and against his legal culpability. Dr Alexander Willson Watt, a specialist at the Royal County Hospital, testified that he thought Hepper was a paranoiac. He said in evidence, 'It is my belief that on the night of 4th February and the morning of 5th February he was prey to his delusions.'

But the prosecution witness, Dr John Matheson, principal medical officer at Brixton prison where the accused had been held on remand awaiting trial, had ample time to examine him and members of his family. He came to the conclusion that Hepper was not, at the time of the crime or since, legally insane.

The jury took under 90 minutes to find him guilty of Margaret Spevik's murder and there can be no doubt that he killed the little girl. But there could be doubt over his mental accountability for the crime – if he was not insane then he had added acting to a list of talents which, by his own account, including having been a successful wool merchant, a translator for the BBC, a spy for the United States, a key figure in the International Brigade during the Spanish Civil War and an exhibiting artist.

Asked if he had anything to say before sentence was passed, the prisoner told the judge, 'I think it is quite unfaithful – I mean, incorrect, I did not do it.' William Hepper went to the gallows on 11th August.

8

POSSESSED BY A GANGSTER

THE MURDER OF JOHN PULL AT DURRINGTON, NOVEMBER 1960

John Henry Pull was a man of many parts and many achievements. His talent as an artist can still be seen in the drawings he made while a pupil at St Andrew's Boys' School, Worthing, before joining the London Rifle Brigade and marching off to the First World War.

He was gassed and taken prisoner, but managed to escape and was still on the run when he learned that the war was over. Many years later his daughter was to recall, 'He wouldn't accept any rank other than private. He found there was so much killing in the war he didn't want to be involved in telling others to kill. He really was a gentle man.'

Shattered by his experiences at the front, he threw himself into a new passion – archaeology. His enthusiasm became so great that he literally took his work home with him. Ancient skeletons were stored under his bed, and he would painstakingly restore bowls and vessels from countless shards of shattered pottery.

Mr Pull carried out pioneering work which made him the acknowledged expert on Stone Age flint-making in the Worthing area. He wrote a book called *The Flint Miners of Blackpatch* about his excavation of the chalk downs near Findon, became Worthing Archaeological

John Pull – digging into the past.

Society's president and even lectured to the Royal Society.

When the Second World War broke out he served in the Home Guard's intelligence unit, based at Muir House in Broadwater, and worked as a postman – Worthing post office was a handy workplace for someone who spent so much of his spare time in the museum opposite.

But the life of one of the town's respected citizens was on a collision course with that of a young man from a completely different background.

Victor John Terry was a 20 year old tearaway with a sinister obsession. He not only identified himself with an infamous American gangster, but also sometimes believed he was possessed by him.

Terry was a product of the Fifties, austere post-war

years which spawned rock and roll and rebellious youth, but his hero came from another age entirely. 'Legs' Diamond was a Chicago gangster of the Twenties, a contemporary of such luminaries as Al 'Scarface' Capone, 'Lucky' Luciano and 'Machine Gun' Kelly. Apart from the affectionate nicknames they gave each other, these gentlemen had one thing in common – violence. Why the youthful Terry picked one of the Mob as his role model is uncertain, but it was an unfortunate choice. Diamond came to a sticky end and the man who emulated him was executed at Wandsworth at dawn on 25th May 1961.

Terry was born in the early years of the Second World War, and grew up in Hounslow, West London. He displayed a complete disregard for the law from an early age. When he was eight he led a gang of equally wild children, some older than himself, on a trail of petty crime. By the age of ten he had his first conviction, and at 18 he was a hardened criminal, sent to Borstal for bludgeoning an old man with a sand-filled sock and stealing £10.

He was by now a drug addict; not heroin or cocaine or sophisticated modern mind-benders, in those days it was 'purple hearts' and amphetamines that captured the minds and bodies of the foolish and self-indulgent in the teenage world of coffee bars, pubs and dance halls.

The worldly-wise city boy with his veneer of sophistication was a big hit with the girls as he drifted south and got himself a job at The Dome dance hall on Worthing's seafront. Like so many before him and since, he found that his 'bad boy' reputation was attractive to the opposite sex. On one occasion the director of The Dome found Terry sitting at a table surrounded by admiring females. He was tossing things up in the air and catching them in his mouth one after the other. An innocent would have used peanuts; he was using purple hearts. A fellow employee was later to admit that he had been getting drugs from a chemist without prescription and supplying them to Terry for some time.

It was in September 1960 that he met and fell for a particularly pretty Worthing girl, aged 18, and she became infatuated with him. She might not, perhaps, have felt so enthusiastic about her Victor had she known he had just ditched a 16 year old who was now pregnant by him.

Terry's criminal career was about to take a more dangerous road. So far his offences had been in the minor bracket and hardly worthy of a desperado like 'Legs' Diamond. Nothing less than a bank raid, of which the gangster would have been proud, would satisfy him now. He made plans and enlisted two childhood cronies to help him carry them out. A 20 year old was taken on to drive the getaway car and promised £200 for his services, while another pal – only 17 – would help with the robbery itself.

Terry announced that he would carry a gun 'to frighten people'. Today it seems incredible that these three young men could calmly wander into a shop in Chiswick on 8th November and buy a shotgun and cartridges for five guineas. Threatening others with a 'liquidator' must have fuelled Terry's imagination. Before, it had only been in his fantasies that he played the mobster with the lethal rod.

In the early hours of 10th November 1960, they stole a Wolseley car in London and headed for Worthing where the gang leader had already checked on likely targets and selected the bank they were to rob. During the journey Terry loaded the gun and shot out of the window at some trees, alarming his 20 year old driver who reminded him that he had promised the gun would only be used to scare their victims. Maybe he was thinking of the youthful Derek Bentley, recently hanged for murdering a policeman though he had never touched a gun in his life. Terry reassured him.

They arrived at his girlfriend's house at 7.30 am and picked her up, carefully hiding the gun so that she would not see it. The foursome then set off for Durrington, to the west of Worthing, with Terry – unnoticed by his girlfriend – continually fiddling with the weapon and mumbling rubbish about being 'the fastest gun in Texas'. As it was a shotgun they had bought, this particular fantasy seems exceptionally bizarre.

At the Durrington branch of Lloyds Bank, young cashier Andrew Baker was behind the counter getting ready to open the bank at 10 am as usual. He was not alone. In the back room was John Henry Pull, now aged 61 and working as a part-time security guard for spare cash. He was making a cup of tea before the day's work began.

The stolen car drew up outside the building. The driver and the girlfriend stayed in their seats while Terry and his accomplice, almost pathetically young but violent and dangerous nonetheless, walked casually into the bank and headed for the safe.

Baker stopped them and asked them what the hell they thought they were doing, and at the same time John Pull came out of the back room still holding a kettle in his left hand. He bravely walked towards the intruders and as he did so he raised his right arm – a peculiar mannerism he had when he was about to speak. Maybe Terry interpreted this as a threatening gesture or thought the guard was armed. Maybe he just wanted to use his new toy. Whatever the reason, he stepped back a pace, produced the single-bore shotgun from under his coat and levelled it at the guard, pulling the trigger at a distance of no more than nine inches.

Mr Pull was hit in the face and died instantly, slumping forward on the floor at the feet of the raiders.

The 17 year old seems to have kept his head better than Terry – at least he remembered what they had come for. He shouted to the cashier and demanded money. Baker, much shocked and understandably frightened, told them where it was and the young accomplice grabbed a Gladstone-type case from behind the counter and headed for the door.

The bungled raid took on an element of horrible farce as the young cashier, still traumatised by what he had just witnessed, shouted out that they had taken the wrong bag. They snatched another and dashed out of the building where the car was waiting with open doors and the engine revving. It screeched away to the sound of the bank's alarm growing fainter in the distance.

The young men soon discovered that their profit for armed robbery and murder was to be pathetically small, but they split up and divided what money there was. The girl was given a share which Terry assured her was for their future home and furniture – she hid it in a bag in her wardrobe after the robbery. Later she was to say that she intended to burn it though this reads rather oddly when set against another of her statements – that she did not think it was a crime to rob a bank!

The hunt for the culprits was immediate and efficient. Terry's accomplices were swiftly netted, arrested while waiting at a bus stop on Worthing seafront with some of the stolen money still in their pockets. But Terry and his girlfriend proved more elusive. That morning they caught a bus to Littlehampton where they stopped at a café for lunch and played the jukebox. From there they hired a taxi to take them to Portsmouth and actually passed a roadblock set up by the police at Chichester – they played the young lovers in the back seat, holding hands, smiling and cuddling. They gave false names and joked that they were getting married in a few days' time and were going on a shopping spree to buy a trousseau.

The girl later told police that this was the first time she knew there had been a killing.

From Portsmouth they took another taxi with the idea of going to the West Country, but at Salisbury they changed their minds and headed back to London where they were dropped off in the Edgware Road. They were only one jump ahead of the police.

The search was nationwide and they were finally cornered in Glasgow where they had booked into a hotel as husband and wife. The publicity given to the case in newspapers and on television alerted the hotel manager who reported to the police his suspicions about a young honeymoon couple staying under his roof. Terry had made two mistakes in trying to shake the law off his tail – he had paid one of the taxi drivers with a ten shilling note for a ride that cost only half-a-crown, and told him to keep the change. And at the hotel he could not resist an act of stupid bravado – he had registered them under the name of Diamond!

Terry stood trial at Lewes Assizes in March 1961, was found guilty of capital murder and sentenced to death. It was claimed by his defence at the trial that his drug-taking world was superimposed by an hallucinatory one in which he was possessed by the spirit of the gangster Diamond and that he heard voices telling him what to do. His appeal against the death sentence failed, and on 23rd May the Home Secretary, Mr R.A. Butler, announced that he had been unable to find sufficient grounds to justify recommending the Queen to interfere with the due course of the law.

The two young accomplices were both found guilty of non-capital murder: the elder was jailed for life, and the younger one to be detained at the Queen's pleasure. They did not appeal.

The girlfriend, accused of harbouring the murderer, was treated sympathetically by the judge who accepted her story that she was both infatuated by and terrified of Victor Terry. She was put on probation for a year and during that same twelve months got engaged to a soldier.

Before Terry's short and violent life came to an abrupt end on the scaffold he learned that he had become a father – the 16 year old girl he had jilted during his dance hall days had borne him a son.

9

MAD DOGS' VENGEANCE

THE MURDER OF CLIVE OLIVE AT SHOREHAM, FEBRUARY 1973

Jim Marshall, as the nation's longest serving detective, probed more than 150 killings in a police career spanning nearly 40 years, but even the hardened Detective Chief Superintendent was not completely prepared for the sight which greeted him on the quayside at Shoreham.

The churning wash of a Dutch cargo ship, negotiating a narrow path out of the harbour, had disturbed the watery grave of Hove teenager Clive Olive. His bound and weighted body, half-eaten by crabs and fishes, had been dumped in the murky depths more than two months earlier. The date of the discovery was Maundy Thursday, 19th April 1973, and it led to one of the biggest murder hunts ever mounted in Sussex.

Hauntingly, detectives found that Olive was still alive when he was beaten, trussed and tossed into the water. With two large breeze-blocks barely heavy enough to drag him down, his head bobbed agonisingly on the moonlit surface, eyes staring accusingly but unseeing. Eight weeks at the mercy of the sea had wreaked its own violence on the remains of the once strapping, swaggering youth. His hands, vital for fingerprint identification, were decaying with the ravages of time,

The victim – Clive 'Ollie' Olive.

salt water and voracious crabs.

Jim Marshall found a moment to reach a phone and ring his wife, Bette. For her, it was a familiar story. 'Don't wait up, love,' he said. 'This is a big case. I could be very late.'

The immediate police problem was a simple one: could they put a name to the rotting corpse? The answer was not long in coming. A palm print the size of a postage

63

stamp, virtually the only skin that survived on one hand, matched with a print kept in the criminal records office at Brighton. The print belonged to Clive Olive, aged 16, who had been reported missing from his home at St Aubyn's, Hove.

The murder trail was already cold – two months had elapsed between the killing and the gruesome discovery, but the investigation led Detective Chief Superintendent Marshall and his team into a new, ugly world dominated by teenage drug takers and violent Hell's Angels chapters.

Lank-haired Ollie was only a youngster, yet he already had a substantial criminal record, boasted about his sexual prowess and used at least six different names. He was also a member of the Sussex Mad Dogs, a Hell's Angels offshoot every bit as sordid as its 'parent' organisation. In many ways the Mad Dogs were the poor relations – unable to afford motorcycles, they roamed on foot.

Ollie's initiation into the local Cougars chapter of the Mad Dogs came on Brighton beach. He removed his jeans and top and allowed every member of the chapter, male and female, to urinate over them. Then he put the clothes back on ... vowing never to wash them. He also had to prove his courage in fights with rival groups before he was awarded his 'colours' and was fully accepted into the chapter.

While the degrading truth about the Mad Dogs was making headlines, police were taking a detailed look at the activities of the young thugs who made up the membership. Mr Marshall was convinced the answer was to be found in the murky, vengeful lifestyle of the Dogs. And he was right.

Trusted detectives who had helped solve other major murder investigations, including one in Hastings immediately prior to the Ollie inquiry, were drafted to specific areas of the case. Two men were sent to the

Midlands to probe Hell's Angels links; another was given the task of making a detailed examination of the cult's twilight lifestyles in Brighton and Hove. Within a week the painstaking inquiry had unearthed dozens of Clive Olive's friends and associates. Few people came forward willingly, but many of Ollie's associates were brought to Hove police station in Holland Road for questioning. As one detective said, 'The murder headquarters looked more like an assembly point for jack-booted Nazi storm-troopers.'

The detailed inquiry threw up many false trails and red herrings. Not the least was a sodden paperback found in Ollie's pocket. The book was *The Maracot Deep*, by Sir Arthur Conan Doyle, which described life at the bottom of the sea. On the front cover was a picture of human bodies languishing on the ocean bed. A chilling irony, indeed, but, as it turned out, of no relevance to the case.

The investigation revealed an overall picture of violence, aggression and degradation among the Mad Dogs and Hell's Angels. Mr Marshall recalled, 'As I read through the statements it made me sick to think of young people wasting their lives on such foul activities. I was glad to leave work, glad to escape into the clean Sussex air.'

Natural revulsion only made Jim Marshall and his team more determined to track down the killers. The big break came when detectives read through the statement of Brian Stephen Moore, a 21 year old member of the Hell's Angels. Moore was interviewed not as a suspect, but as part of the police 'sweep' to speak with anyone even remotely connected with the dead boy. His statement described in vivid detail how Moore had overheard a gang of three Angels from outside who were plotting to get Olive. Moore said he even heard his own name mentioned by the mystery gang. The chance eavesdropping seemed too much of a coincidence and

Brian Moore – proud of his White Hunter uniform.

the thought immediately occurred that perhaps it was an elaborate cover story to send detectives on a false trail. Jim Marshall and his senior officers, reading through the many hundreds of statements being collected from all corners of the country, decided to have a closer look at Brian Moore.

Moore, a former zoo-keeper now working as a cleaner, lived with his parents in Pankhurst Avenue, Brighton. Also living at the same address was his pregnant sister Christine, then 18, and her husband Albert Dorn, 27, a labourer known as Mouse or Little Al because of his height. Significantly, all three were either current or past members of Hell's Angels chapters, and all three knew Clive Olive. Descriptions of a black van believed used in connection with the killing also matched a vehicle recently bought by Dorn, but there was an even more damning connection. Moore had discovered that his pretty 16 year old girlfriend had allegedly been raped by Ollie . . . and he vowed to settle the score.

Police were by now convinced that Moore had made up the story about a Hell's Angels 'hit squad'. At first, all three denied any connection with Ollie's death but Moore, outwardly the toughest of them all, eventually cracked under questioning. Desperately he clutched at the hand of a detective and whispered, 'Please help me. You've got to help me.'

He told the story of how he had beaten Ollie senseless in the back of Dorn's van after luring him with talk of a drugs deal. 'I asked him what had happened with the girl and he got all mouthy. I lost my temper with him . . . I've got a terrible temper.'

He added, 'I don't know how many times I hit him but his head just slumped forward. I didn't want to touch him so I lifted up his head with a truncheon I carried with me. His eyes were all staring. It was diabolical. I've had nightmares about those staring eyes.'

Albert Dorn was driving the van and his wife Christine was in the front seat. Albert helped Moore dump the body but his wife took no active part in the horror. Both Moore and Dorn described to police the moment they tipped Ollie's living body into the water. Moore said, 'We both thought he was dead, but after we threw him in he just bobbled about in the water and when he went down there were loads of bubbles. We wondered then if he was still alive. I've told you, it was the eyes that got me.'

Later Dorn described how he had tried to cover up the dreadful crime by getting rid of the truncheon for Moore and dumping a bloodstained carpet and seat from the back of the van.

Police who went to the Dorns' bedroom were shocked

Left to right Christine Dorn, Frank 'Wank' Smith and Shaun 'Tramp' Keevil.

by what they found. It was decorated with souvenirs and posters about the Hell's Angels and was festooned with swastikas and portraits of Adolf Hitler. Mr Marshall said, 'I wondered about the future of their baby if it was to be brought up in such menacing surroundings.'

The court case began on 26th November 1973, before an all-male jury at Lewes. All three denied murder and dozens of Hell's Angels packed the heavily guarded public gallery. Moore's own defence counsel, making an impassioned plea for diminished responsibility, said of his bearded client, 'He nurtured an obsession with all the cunning of a maniac – and killed with the remorseless cruelty of a maniac.'

After a trial lasting a little over eight days, the jury took seven hours to deliver their verdicts: Moore and Albert 'Mouse' Dorn were both guilty of murder; Christine Dorn was not guilty of murder but guilty of manslaughter. Moore and Dorn were jailed for life. Christine Dorn received ten years but was later released when her conviction was quashed by the Appeal Court.

There was one other twist to the Ollie murder. On the evening of the arrests, the murder team held a 'debriefing' in the social club bar at Hove police station. Gifts were exchanged and, by tradition, senior officers stood for a round of drinks. For Jim Marshall, the celebration was interrupted by the telephone. 'There's been another murder, this time at Seaford,' said the voice from headquarters. 'Can you go, sir?'

There was just time for one more call. 'Is that you love?' Detective Chief Superintendent Marshall said to his wife. 'Don't wait up for me . . . I'm going to be late again.'

10

DEATH IN THE GRAVEYARD

THE MURDER OF JOHANNA HARRIMAN AT WEST TARRING, DECEMBER 1979

Late on the evening of Friday, 28th December 1979, horrific screams were heard in the churchyard of St Andrew's church at West Tarring.

There were four in all, ending in 'a very deep sobbing sound'. Keith Crowley and his wife Sheila, whose home in Church Road overlooked the tombstones, had just got into bed. He pulled on his dressing gown, armed himself with a poker and went out into the stormy night to investigate. He crossed the road to the entrance to the churchyard but, hearing nothing more, went back indoors to bed. About five minutes later the couple heard more sobbing. 'It lasted for two or three minutes before it slowly died away,' recalled Mrs Crowley.

They were later to discover that they had been hearing the last desperate moments in the life of 22 year old Johanna Harriman. Her partially clothed body was found in the churchyard four days later, hidden by leaves and branches. She had been mercilessly battered and kicked to death.

Slim brunette Johanna was a mixture of homely girl and fashion-conscious young woman. The working week was spent in the typing pool of Charlesworth Motor Policies at Lloyds, in Teville Gate, where she was well thought of.

Murder victim – Johanna Harriman.

She was quiet and conscientious at work and stayed in most evenings with her parents. But when she went out, usually to pubs near her home in Ely Road, she got noticed. On the night she died she was wearing a sexy black dress with a split up the side and a white imitation sheepskin jacket.

She was probably unaware of the effect this might have, and unable to handle a situation that got out of hand. Her mother, Shirley Harriman, said 'She was a quiet, shy sort of girl and lived for her home and her work as a typist. She had few friends and no boyfriends. She was not a worldly sort of girl and was not the type that would be invited twice to parties.'

She was a girl of habit. Saturday mornings she spent shopping, ending her trips to Worthing town centre with lunch at the British Home Stores restaurant. Then the usual routine was to return home and watch sport on television with her invalid father, Mr Louis Harriman.

Johanna Harriman's bedroom, with her pet cat, Paddy, on the window sill.

Later she would don her smart clothes and go out for the evening, usually drinking alone and happy to watch other people enjoying themselves, at The Golden Lion in Durrington or The Swan in the town centre. She had no regular boyfriend, but she wanted one. Johanna always returned home about 11 pm and her mother would leave sandwiches and a flask of coffee for her in the kitchen.

Her great love was music, with a collection of modern hits and a record player in her bedroom. She was also a talented pianist from her days at a Broadstairs boarding school, and had made an impression at several music festivals. Posters of Snoopy vied for space on her bedroom wall with James Dean and Elvis Presley, and she was devoted to her pet cat Paddy.

Johanna had been adopted by Mr and Mrs Harriman as a baby and brought up as a Roman Catholic. It was the couple's strong religious convictions that were to help them through the ordeal that lay ahead.

With Christmas and Boxing Day gone, the former beauty contest competitor changed her routine and went to The North Star pub. She got there at about 9 pm and soon got into conversation with a stranger.

Builder's labourer Albert Edward Stanley was a 28 year old with a long list of previous convictions which included two offences of assault occasioning actual bodily harm and one of having sex with a girl under the age of 16. He was known as 'Randy' by his drinking cronies. Married, with three children, he lived in a council house at Chiltern Crescent, Durrington. As the evening wore on the conversation between Johanna and Stanley became more intimate and several people in the crowded North Star bar saw the couple kissing and cuddling. They left the pub together at closing time.

The following day Johanna's worried parents reported her missing, and 'Randy' Stanley was offering her ring, watch and cigarette lighter for sale in The North Star.

The North Star pub where Johanna Harriman had her fateful meeting with 'Randy' Stanley.

The anguish of uncertainty ended for Mr and Mrs Harriman on 2nd January when their daughter's body was found under the branches and leaves at the southern perimeter of the graveyard – a mere 500 yards from her home. Her body was unclothed from the waist down. Stockings, shoes and other items of her clothing were scattered in the graveyard. She had died from multiple injuries to her head and neck consistent with being struck a series of violent blows or kicks. The cause of death was inhalation of her own blood, and her injuries included fractures to the jaw, nose and larynx. There was no evidence that sexual intercourse had taken place.

Finding the person responsible was hardly a mystery. The police went straight to Stanley as the last person seen with Johanna, though he strenuously denied murder. He initially claimed he had never seen the possessions he offered for sale, but later said he stole them from a car at High Salvington. Later still he changed his story to say that he bought them from the dead girl for £7, although they were worth at least £50.

When the case came before Lewes Crown Court in October, Mr Roger Gray QC, prosecuting, told the jury, 'The picture you may frame in your mind is of a young girl battered mercilessly to death by a murderer whose sexual passion was aroused.'

Mr Gray was merciless himself with Stanley. The events following closing time in The North Star, when witnesses had seen the couple together, were the point of his attack. Questioned about part-time barman Andrew Taylor's sighting of Stanley and Johanna outside the lychgate of St Andrew's church late that evening, the accused said that Mr Taylor was not telling the truth. Asked what he had to say about other witnesses who saw him kissing and cuddling Johanna, Stanley replied they must have been mistaken.

'Was Mrs Teresa Churcher mistaken or giving wrong evidence when she said she saw you and the girl kissing?' asked Mr Gray.

'I can't remember,' said Stanley.

'Have you got a very bad memory?'

'Yes, I have.'

Stanley said he had left Johanna at the bus stop and then walked home. When told the driver of the 206 bus said he had not picked up any passengers in Littlehampton Road that night, Stanley replied that the driver must have been lying.

The court heard that the dead girl's handbag had been found stuffed down a drain at a spot in Salvington Road near Stanley's home where he had been seen walking at 1 am. He did admit to buying Johanna a drink at The North Star, though he denied kissing her and putting his arm round her. He had consumed about seven pints of lager that evening, which was a rarity. He usually drank about twelve pints, he told the court.

A policewoman wearing a coat identical to Johanna's during the investigation.

Stanley showed no emotion on the eighth day of the trial when the jury returned after two hours and 40 minutes with a unanimous verdict of guilty. Mr Justice Milmo told him, 'You have been convicted of the crime of murder on evidence that was overwhelming. There is only one sentence that I can pass on you and that is you should be imprisoned for life.'

Stanley's wife, Vivienne, was not in court to hear the verdict, but one of his sisters and an aunt were sitting in the public gallery and both women later stood sobbing outside the court. Aunt Mrs Unity Ayres said, 'I never believed he did it. As long as I live I'll never believe he did it.'

11

THE *IT'S A KNOCKOUT* MURDER INVESTIGATION

THE MANSLAUGHTER OF JONATHAN LEWIS AT ARUNDEL, AUGUST 1980

It was meant to be a magical occasion for Sussex, a prestigious night when six million pairs of eyes across the globe would be focused on the county. *It's A Knockout*, or *Jeux Sans Frontieres*, was a game show at its peak when the Arun district successfully staked a claim to host the British heat. The theme was 'magic' for the contestants across the Continent who gathered at the Avisford Park Hotel at Walburton near Arundel on the night of 23rd July 1980. Giant toppers, wands, dice, playing cards and, of course, jokers, dominated proceedings calculated to be remembered as one of the best *Knockouts* ever. But behind the façade of midsummer jollity lurked a love triangle, deceit and death.

The Arun team, carrying the flag for Britain, was defeated in the arena, but the show was hailed as a great success. Praise was showered on the sponsors, Arun District Council, and particularly on the local authority's information and liaison officer, Colin Wallace, who had led the backroom team which masterminded the event. His *Knockout* colleagues included tourism officers Ned Wayne and Tony Baker, and his vivacious, dark-haired assistant, Jane Lewis.

The 37 year old Ulsterman and his pretty sidekick had

been brought close together by the organisation and planning. So close, that a romantic relationship had developed – though both maintained that it had stopped short of adultery. They had happy marriages to nurture. Colin's wife Eileen was a great organiser, who had gained the post of secretary to the Duke of Norfolk at Arundel Castle in the four years her husband had been employed by the district council, while Jane, 27, had been married barely a year to antiques dealer Jonathan Lewis, 29, who had a shop in Brighton's famous Lanes. The two couples had made a foursome on the local social scene... which made the clandestine relationship between Wallace and his assistant all the more awkward.

He organised two dinners at the Avisford Park Hotel to celebrate the Eurovision success, and to thank all those who had made it so. Jonathan and Jane Lewis could not attend the first because they were celebrating their wedding anniversary alone together, but they were eagerly awaiting the second, on the evening of Tuesday, 5th August.

Jane, after an early evening game of squash with Eileen, was surprised and delighted to find that she was given the place of honour as principal guest. She chatted happily with the prominent individuals who had helped with *Knockout* and, though her husband's place beside her remained empty, she was not unduly worried. He was due to arrive separately, coming straight from a busy day at work. Colin said he had received a telephone call from Jonathan earlier in the evening warning that he might arrive late because of another appointment.

Jane ordered a meal for him but it was never eaten. She began to grow anxious, and telephone calls were made to their home in Ferndale Walk, Angmering, and Jonathan's warehouse at Portslade. Neither produced an answer.

The non-arrival threw a black cloud over the evening, which was added to when Wallace, the host, had to

Colin Wallace and Jane Lewis.

excuse himself from the meal, suffering from a minor stomach disorder. He disappeared for about 40 minutes while he went to collect some tablets from his home in Dalloway Road, Arundel. It was a minor enough event at the time, but was to prove of great interest to the police later.

When the party broke up at about midnight, Jane rushed home and began ringing friends, particularly in the antiques world, to see if they had heard from Jonathan. It is some measure of the respect in which he was held as 'an honest dealer' that twelve colleagues in the trade took the next day off work to help locate him.

Three agonising days passed before any concrete news emerged. The missing man's distinctive orange Volvo was found in the car park at Arundel swimming pool. The discovery prompted Wallace and Jane Lewis to tell a senior police friend at Arundel about their secret affair.

At the same time two teenage boys in a speedboat spotted what looked like a head in the water as they made their way up the river Arun towards the Black Rabbit pub at Arundel. They summoned the help of a local fisherman and were appalled to discover that it was indeed a body. With difficulty, it was towed about a mile down river to be brought ashore at Ford Marina. Even as Wallace and Jane were talking to their police friend the news of the discovery came in, and Jane was gently taken aside and told that her husband's body had been found in the river.

A theory that Jonathan had accidentally fallen into the Arun and drowned was swiftly discounted by the pathologist, who discovered that the victim had a fractured skull and a gash to the forehead – fatal injuries caused certainly before immersion in the water. Robbery was not the motive, because £203 was found in a trouser pocket.

Police found an intriguing entry in the dead man's diary for 5th August. It read simply: 'Colin 6.30 pm'. An

Austin Princess car decked out in *'It's A Knockout'* stickers and the Union Jack had been seen at this time in the vicinity of the swimming pool car park. Four had been supplied during the recording of the TV show. Only Colin Wallace was still at the wheel of the car he had been loaned.

Inevitably suspicion fell on him. He told police that he and Jonathan Lewis were on good terms and that the entry in the dead man's diary referred simply to one of their regular games of squash, which they had decided to cancel. But when informed by the police that a *Knockout* courtesy car had been spotted in the pool car park at that time and a man answering his description had been seen to meet another man beside an orange Volvo, Wallace took a long pause and told a completely different story. Jonathan had confronted him about the relationship with his wife, but there had been no heated argument. Wallace had said he was seeking a job elsewhere before things got out of hand, and the two men parted on amicable terms.

The dead man's watch and his missing car keys were found near the sluice gates at the end of Gasworks Lane, a rough track leading to the river's edge, where marks on the steep bank suggested a body might have slid down to the water to be pushed to and fro by the tide five times before its discovery.

A second post mortem revealed Jonathan had suffered a further unusual injury. His nose had been rammed backwards and upwards by a fierce blow, cracking the front of his skull. If he was alive when he slid into the water, the normally strong swimmer would have been severely concussed.

Forensic tests of Wallace's car revealed considerable evidence of blood stains in the boot and, on 19th September, the day the recorded *It's A Knockout* was broadcast, the public relations man was brought before Arundel Magistrates Court and charged with the murder of his friend Jonathan Lewis.

When the case came before Lewes Crown Court Dan Hollis QC, prosecuting, alleged Wallace had planned the killing because of his love for Jonathan Lewis's wife. He had lured the antiques dealer to his home in Dalloway Road, having carefully made sure that both their wives were playing squash, and then knocked him unconscious with a violent blow. He had dragged the body through the house and stuffed it into the boot of his car, driven to Gasworks Lane and pushed the helpless victim down the concrete-lined bank into the fast-flowing river. Hollis suggested this might have taken place between 7 pm and 8 pm as Wallace was preparing to join his guests for dinner, or under the cover of darkness at 10.30 pm when he had made an excuse to leave the table.

The accused man strongly denied the allegations throughout, even though Jane Lewis's affection had turned to suspicion. Michael Kennedy QC, defending, said anyone could have carried out the attack. Maybe the groggy victim had staggered down to the water's edge, then fallen in and drowned.

The forensic information became vital in the case. A minute spot of what might have been blood was found in the upstairs lavatory of Wallace's home, but the blood of more than one person – including Lewis's rare grouping – was found in the car boot. Three assembly workers from the British Leyland plant at Cowley told the court they had all sustained cuts while assembling the Austin Princess in June 1979, and blood from at least one of them might have found its way into the crucial boot area.

The judge, Mr Justice Kilner Brown, caused a sensation when he instructed that there was insufficient evidence to continue on a murder charge. There was a thin dividing line in his reasoning: to put an unconscious man in the water so he drowns is murder; to put a man you believed to be dead in the water was manslaughter.

The trial lasted 13 days and the jury took four and a half hours to reach a unanimous verdict – guilty of manslaughter. The judge told Wallace: 'This was a dreadful case, a horrifying case. There was a perfectly innocent man, a man on the verge of being cuckolded by you and that man received these savage blows. It may well be that you believed he was dead. It may well be that you could not care one way or the other. In my judgement one has got to recognise that there has never been an attempt to explain what happened. The very notion of driving that body and tipping it into the river revolts the human consciousness. As manslaughter goes, in my experience, it is one of the worst cases I have come across.'

Wallace was jailed for ten years. He did not spend them idly. After his appeal failed he served only five years behind bars as a model prisoner and launched a campaign to clear his name with the steadfast support of his wife Eileen, who stoutly defended his innocence. Both maintained he had been framed to gag him . . . because he knew too much.

As a former senior information officer with the British Army – dismissed in 1975 for passing on a sensitive military document to a journalist – he had vital knowledge of the notorious Clockwork Orange campaign of the 1970s, the shadowy world of 'dirty tricks' said to have included the undermining not only of the forces of terrorism in Northern Ireland but also of numerous leading British politicians. Wallace said he had been deliberately discredited to prevent him spreading his vital knowledge.

He built up a massive dossier in prison and, though denials flowed from Whitehall, he had influential friends in Parliament who were prepared to bombard the Commons with questions. Eventually, documents came to light which convinced some senior members of the

Civil Service that Wallace was not the 'Walter Mitty' character he had been branded.

In 1990 Prime Minister Margaret Thatcher was forced to make a statement in which she said previous denials were incorrect and Armed Forces Minister Archie Hamilton confirmed that 'inaccurate statements' had been made in the Commons. It was conceded that psychological warfare had existed against terrorism, although not against politicians.

After an extensive investigation by Thomas Calcutt QC, it was concluded that Wallace's dismissal from the Army had been 'unsatisfactory', and he was awarded £30,000 in compensation. He had emerged as a cog in the cloak-and-dagger machine, part of a unit which apparently specialised in the spreading of black propaganda.

Having established credibility on the political front, Wallace has continued to try and clear his name of manslaughter. In 1990 the Home Office decided there were no fresh grounds to justify a new investigation.

12

THE FOREST TORSO

THE MURDER OF LATIFA LAZAAR AT CRAWLEY, AUGUST 1986

It was early on Sunday 31st August 1986 that a driver pulled into a wooded lay-by off the busy A22 London to Eastbourne road. Ashdown Forest, vast and beautiful, surrounded him, but he was about to make a hideous discovery. Fifteen yards from the road between Nutley and Wych Cross two bundles were buried in shallow graves. Inside, mutilated and beyond recognition, were human remains. One of the most difficult murder hunts ever undertaken in the county had begun.

Police had little to go on. The victim had literally been skinned and chopped to pieces, and the head and internal organs were missing. Detectives not only had to find the killer, they also had to establish who had been killed. Painstakingly, the murder team managed to build a sparse picture. The body was that of a woman. She was 5 feet 3 inches tall, aged between 18 and 35, had given birth, had a deformed rib cage and a vaginal scar. Much later, it was revealed she died of a cut throat.

Detective Superintendent Bryan Grove, leading the hunt, contemplated using an aircraft with heat-seeking equipment to fly over the huge county council rubbish tip at Faygate. He thought the head might have been dumped there. Experts looked into the possibility of excavating the tip – a task equal to looking for the proverbial needle in a haystack. Despite Mr Grove's pleas, excavation was ruled out.

Fifty police officers examined information from nearly 800 people. More than 130 missing wives, daughters and girlfriends were checked. The grisly remains had been wrapped in curtains, which were featured on the BBC *Crimewatch UK* programme on 18th September. A woman thought she recognised her herringbone stitches on the altered hem of the blue curtain found wrapped around the torso; she had sold it at a car boot sale at Crawley station.

It was the sort of lead detectives desperately needed. The murder squad, based at East Grinstead, decided to concentrate its efforts on Crawley, north Sussex and south Surrey. The manufacturers and distributors of the curtains were traced.

Just when the trail appeared to have run cold, all the publicity surrounding the case caused a man to panic. Kassem Lachaal went to his solicitors and asked them to write to Crawley police. The letter said Latifa Lazaar had left her Crawley home and had been due to return to her native Morocco, but she had not arrived there. Lachaal feared that she might be the murder victim and he was concerned that suspicion might fall on him. The letter proved to be the breakthrough the police needed. They now had a possible name for the headless torso and a prime suspect in the shape of Kassem Lachaal.

Detectives checked medical records and found that Latifa had undergone operations for a vaginal abscess and a thyroid complaint. They also discovered she had a conviction for shoplifting and details on her criminal record matched the woman so carefully 'reconstructed' by Home Office pathologist Dr Michael Heath when the butchered corpse was found. Convinced they were on the right track, police swooped on Latifa's home in Ramsey Court, part of the huge Broadfield estate on the western edge of Crawley – and entered the tangled

The victim – Latifa Lazaar. The curtains behind became her shroud.

world of an evil Romeo with a string of affairs behind him.

Under Moslem law, Moroccan Lachaal was allowed more than one wife. One of them was Fatima, aged 40, who was arrested with him, and it emerged that the other was the murder victim, 25 year old Latifa Lazaar. The police took away bags of material for forensic tests. Photographic probes were used to search the drains around the house and neighbours were questioned. Significantly, the tiny bathroom was taken apart.

In December 1986, the investigation net spread more than 1,000 miles to Morocco. Detectives visited Latifa and Lachaal's home town of Metnes and spent five days interviewing both families. Blood samples were taken from her 55 year old widowed mother, her brother and two sisters and brought back to England for DNA tests. Time had taken its toll – the blood from the hacked torso had deteriorated too much for scientists to tell if it came from the same family, but the police were convinced. Lachaal and Fatima were charged with murder, though they claimed Latifa had gone back to Africa to divorce him.

Pretty Latifa was not alone in falling under the spell of 'lady's man' Lachaal. Tall and well-groomed, he was well known for his Casanova charms. Though married to Fatima, he had relationships with at least half a dozen other women, including a mother and her teenage daughter. In 1981 he had threatened to slit a schoolgirl's throat if she quit their illegal love affair. He took the girl to Worth Abbey Woods, told her to take her clothes off and warned her not to leave him, allegedly telling her, 'I will cut your neck and cut you into little pieces. It will be the perfect murder.' The girl became pregnant and returned to Morocco where she had an abortion. She rang police anonymously after Lachaal was arrested and they managed to trace her.

Latifa's ill-fated link with Sussex and Lachaal began with an arranged marriage to another man in Morocco in 1980. While in the town of Metnes, the petite, dark-haired 19 year old married Beniassa Lamnour. The couple moved from North Africa to Crawley, and within three months Lachaal had worked his charms on the young bride and they began an illicit affair.

Both kept it a secret from their partners and the two

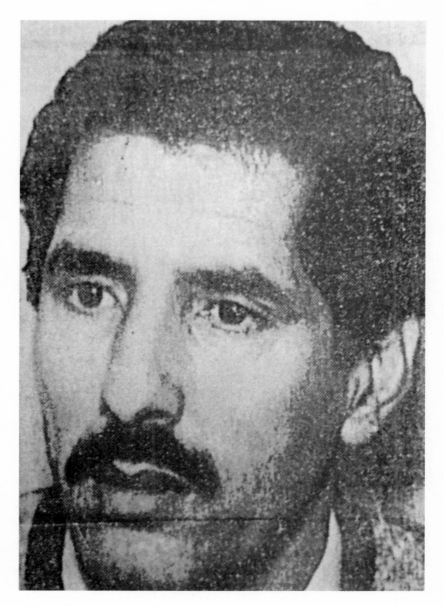

The killer – Kassem Lachaal.

couples were all friends. They even went on holiday together to Morocco. It was a stormy trip – Beniassa and Latifa rowed, divorced and then remarried each other only days later. Life at their council home in Ramsey Court was seldom calm, and they soon had a young son, Ashraf, to support. Latifa went to her doctor at least five times suffering from bruises. On one occasion she also had a broken arm.

The storm broke when Beniassa returned home early from work one day and found the front door locked. As he peered through the letterbox he saw Lachaal scamper down the stairs. Beniassa threatened him with a kitchen chopper, but Latifa was good at covering her tracks and her husband almost believed her when she said nothing was going on. As final proof, he demanded Lachaal swear on the holy Koran that there was no affair. He refused.

It meant the end of a four year marriage. Beniassa returned to Morocco in June 1984 and divorced Latifa. She continued to live in Ramsey Court and see Lachaal, both as workmates at APV in Crawley and as lovers. He would stay with her at Ramsey Court at weekends. At other times, she slept with him at the nearby Greenwich Close, Crawley, home that Lachaal shared with his wife Fatima and five children. The love triangle and Lachaal's reputation as a lady's man were no secret in Crawley's tightly-knit Moroccan community. Men disliked him because they feared he might become involved with their wives.

When Latifa asked him to marry her, he agreed. In August 1985, the couple went to Morocco and wed while Fatima stayed at home in Crawley to look after the children. The honeymoon was brief. The ferry from Dieppe docked at Newhaven on 25th August, 1985. Lachaal's car was stopped and cannabis was found in a suitcase. At Lewes Crown Court the following February he denied smuggling 7.75 kilograms of the drug worth

£17,000 into Britain, but was convicted and sentenced to 18 months in prison.

With their husband behind bars, Latifa and her 'sister wife' lived together with the children in Greenwich Close. Fatima gave up her job as a mushroom-picker because Latifa could not cope with six children at once. Fatima was later to deny that there was any jealousy between the two women. It was suggested by the prosecution at the murder trial at Lewes Crown Court that Latifa was the 'younger, sexier' wife, but Fatima – showing a rare display of emotion – retorted, 'I'm pretty. I'm not ugly.'

The 'younger, sexier' wife was under the impression that Lachaal would take her away when he was released from prison. She told a friend that they were going to buy a house and live together in Brighton.

Lachaal's homecoming coincided with the Moslem Sacrifice of Lamb feast. Latifa went shopping and bought him a new jumper, as well as presents and cards for the children to give him. He arrived home on 13th August, a day earlier than expected. On Friday, 15th August, the day of the feast, a friend saw Lachaal and Latifa, both looking happy. She was dressed up, had make-up on and had a new hair-do. The next day, Saturday 16th August, was the last time she was seen alive except by her killer.

Exactly what happened between that date and the gruesome discovery at Ashdown Forest remains cloudy. Even the judge at the 18 day trial in March 1988, Mr Justice Farquharson, told Fatima, 'I feel we have not learned everything about the facts in this case or your part in it.'

The court heard how Lachaal carried out one of the county's most callous and grisly murders. He took Latifa to the bathroom of the Ramsey Court home and slit her throat. Then, with Fatima, he undertook an elaborate cover-up. He spent several hours cutting up and skinning the body in the bath in an attempt to prevent identification. The butchering would have taken many hours and it appeared a blunt knife had been used. The head, arms and lower legs were removed and found in the forest. Her skull, teeth and fingers were found by chance 18 months later near Worth Abbey. Some parts of her body have never been found.

It took the jury six hours and 46 minutes to find Lachaal guilty of killing his young wife, and he was given a life sentence. He showed no emotion as the jury returned its ten to two majority verdict, but Fatima wept quietly. She was cleared of murder, but found guilty on a similar majority verdict of trying to help conceal the crime and was sentenced to 18 months imprisonment. However, the judge took into account the amount of time she had already spent in custody and she walked free four days later.

It was the letter to the police protesting innocence which proved Lachaal's undoing. If he had kept his nerve through the glare of publicity and anxious questions from his missing wife's family and friends, if he had not tried to clear his name, police might never have identified the pathetic remains in Ashdown Forest.

After the trial the new tenant of Number 5, Ramsey Court, confessed to reporters that she could not bear to sleep there, preferring to cross the town and spend the night with her parents. She said, 'I know what happened there and it's horrible and creepy; it frightens me too much.'

13

BABES IN
THE WOOD

THE MURDERS OF KAREN HADAWAY AND
NICOLA FELLOWS AT BRIGHTON, OCTOBER 1986

Almost 200 police and as many neighbours searched the rambling acres of wilderness known as Brighton's Wild Park. A police helicopter clattered into view, hovered for a moment, and then swept low and fast over the rough terrain. All were hunting for any clue which would lead them to missing nine year olds Karen Hadaway and Nicola Fellows. It was Friday, 10th October 1986, and the start of one of the most harrowing cases in the annals of crime in Sussex.

When the girls were found it at first appeared they were still alive, huddled together for warmth. Then, as more police arrived on the scene, the truth became only too obvious. The schoolgirl friends, both from the tough Moulscomb estate just a short distance away, had been brutally murdered.

Such was the nature of the murders that police later spared the parents the worst of the details. It was a necessary kindness. Nicola Fellows had been sexually assaulted both before and after she was murdered. She had also been hit in the face. Karen Hadaway's clothing had been disturbed and there were signs, too, that she had been sexually assaulted. Both children had been strangled. Their bodies were covered in bruises and

93

scratches. Nicola was lying on her back near the opening to a secluded den in the middle of the wood. Karen's body was close by, her head resting on Nicola's lap. Both families lived in Newick Road, a few minutes' walk from Wild Park, and the girls had known each other virtually since birth. Nicola's last words to her mother had been, 'I'm just going across the road. I won't be long.'

Only Lee and Michelle Hadaway, and Barrie Fellows and his wife, Susan, know how they felt on that fateful evening when the grim news finally came through that their daughters were dead. The whole sprawling estate, considered the poor relation of Brighton, rallied round in support of the shattered families. There was anger and sympathy, hatred and concern.

Both families had spent much of the day helping the searchers. So had Russell Bishop, the father of two, who eventually stood in the dock accused of the killings. It was 21 year old Bishop who had confirmed to Mrs Hadaway that her daughter was dead.

Three weeks after the killings, Bishop was arrested by detectives and questioned for 51 hours before being released on bail. He went into hiding and police guarded his empty council flat in Stephens Road, Hollingdean. He was charged with the killings on 3rd December and appeared in court at Hove the following day, where magistrates decided that he should stand trial at Lewes Crown Court.

Why had police attention focused on Bishop, the volunteer searcher? He claimed to have seen the bodies during the search of Wild Park's sprawling acres, and told police how the bodies were lying. But they said he never got close enough and detectives suspected he knew the details because he was the killer.

Bishop lived in fear in London's Brixton prison as he awaited trial. He feared fellow inmates would lace his food with deadly additives such as broken glass because of the severity of the charges against him, so restricted his diet to digestive biscuits and Kit-Kats. The only real nourishment he got was when family and friends brought hampers containing fresh fruit and nuts.

The youngest of five brothers, he had attended Coldean School, Brighton, where staff realised he had a problem with learning and behaviour. He was found to be slightly educationally subnormal and, when he was 14, he was diagnosed as dyslexic. He went to a special Catholic school in Worcester and then returned to Sussex where he attended St Mary's day and residential school at Horam, near Heathfield. He could not settle as a boarder at the East Sussex County Council school and soon took to running away and hitch-hiking to Brighton. He was taken away from St Mary's and from the age of 16 had private tuition from family friend Angela Sanders.

After he had been charged with the murders his mother, Mrs Sylvia Bishop, said she had received scores of letters from people 'totally convinced' that her son was innocent. 'The phone never stopped ringing,' she said. 'But we never had one hate letter or call. He is a popular lad around the estate and he's lived here all his life.' Family friend Barbara Gibbons described him as 'a bit of a romancer, a dreamer. He makes things up, but there's no harm in that until it gets you into trouble.'

It was a different story from that of the father of victim Nicola Fellows, who figured as much in the Wild Park inquiry as the man accused of the killings. Barrie Fellows, 36, had been interviewed at length by the police. He had a past – as a young man, he led a life of petty crime which landed him in jail. He was convicted of deception, burglary and receiving stolen goods. Two years before his daughter's death he was in the news again, promoting and showing pornographic video films.

During the trial of Bishop much was made of the fact that while others were out hunting for Nicola on the

Russell Bishop.

night she disappeared, her father calmly sat down to eat his supper rather than join the search. Mr Fellows' answer was that there was no immediate worry as she often went missing. Public opinion, fuelled by vicious rumour, ran high. When he and his wife Susan were about to move from their Newick Road home to another part of the Moulscomb estate they fell victim to a hateful attack. Cruel graffiti on the walls of their new home declared, 'Fellows out. You're a murderer and a child molester and a child killer.' The family braved the storm, moving instead just a few doors away to a former home of Nicola's playmate, Karen.

While Bishop awaited trial, his common-law wife, Jenny Johnson – mother of his two children Victor and Hayley – stood by him and announced that she planned to marry him. Their relationship had been anything but idyllic. They frequently rowed, late at night and in public. Things got so bad that one resident of the couple's Stephens Road block of flats organised a petition to get rid of them. Most people refused to sign it. They had lived in their two-bedroom flat for about 18 months before the killings. Stubborn Jenny made Bishop do his own washing, a fact he hid from close friends and neighbours for fear of ridicule.

The seething emotions of a rough, tough council estate – where all strangers were treated with cold suspicion during the murder investigation – came to a head at the end of Bishop's four-week trial at Lewes Crown Court in December 1987.

A jury of eight women and four men took just over two hours to find him not guilty of murdering the schoolgirls in what had been dubbed 'The Babes in the Wood Murders'. Bishop sobbed in the dock as his family and friends erupted into cheers and clapping. In the public gallery Lee Hadaway buried his face in his hands. He and his wife Michelle left the court together in tears. Members of the family of Barrie Fellows, Nicola's father, said he could not bring himself to be at court that day.

After the verdict, a Sussex Police spokesman said, 'This case was thoroughly investigated by us at the time. No new information emerged during the trial and we have no plans to reopen this inquiry. But obviously any fresh information which was put to us would be carefully looked at.'

Five years later, Russell Bishop was jailed for life for abducting and assaulting a nine year old girl at the Devil's Dyke beauty spot on the Downs near Brighton.

14

DOUBLE DEATH

THE MURDER OF STEPHEN AND IRIS HADLER AT NEWHAVEN, JULY 1989

Imagine the worst nightmare of two elderly and disabled people living on their own. It happened to devoted couple Stephen and Iris Hadler. Their double murder in the summer of 1989 shocked the county and sickened hardened policemen. Detective Superintendent Chris Page, who led the investigation, described the killings as 'absolutely horrific'.

Mr and Mrs Hadler had led a blameless and productive life. In the twilight of their years, they were happy to live quietly in their terraced home in Gibbon Road, Newhaven, and keep the modest garden immaculate. It was the most they could do. Stephen, at 72, was an invalid. He had suffered a stroke 16 years earlier but though partially paralysed had continued to work as a highly respected member of East Sussex County Council's education department, based at County Hall in Lewes. Iris, two years his senior, was frail and becoming senile. Neighbours remember them as happy and cheerful – Mr Hadler was kind and intelligent and Mrs Hadler was described as 'angelic' – but they liked to keep themselves to themselves.

All that changed on the hot Friday night of 21st July. The couple, wearing only their nightclothes, were later discovered in pools of blood in a bedroom of their home after being stabbed repeatedly. The wounds indicated that Stephen had put up a brave fight to defend them both and, even more ghastly, that his wife had been sexually assaulted. A knife was found near the bodies.

Police launched a massive hunt for the killer of the innocent old couple. It was a warm summer, but they urged all elderly people and anyone living on their own to ensure that all ground floor windows were kept closed and locked at night. It was a worrying time for old folks, especially as police had not ruled out the possibility that the frenzied attack was linked with a string of recent assaults on elderly women in Eastbourne and north Sussex.

Detective Superintendent Page stressed that the attacker 'was a very dangerous man' and anyone sharing a house with him would know he was responsible because his clothing would have been heavily bloodstained. In fact, the man they were searching for was a loner. But he made a mistake which finally led to his conviction.

The search for the killer covered a wide area but it was less than a month old and less than a mile from the scene of the crime when the police found what they were looking for – one of the dead man's shirts. It was in the caravan home of building site worker Denis Harland Roberts, a 41 year old driller from Birkenhead, Merseyside, who had come south to find work in the construction industry. He was living on the windswept Downland Caravan Park, in Court Farm Road, Newhaven.

On his own admission he had picked the shirt up as he left from the back of the Page's house in Gibbon Road. But robbery was his only motive, the court heard, and he strenuously denied murder. The front door of the pensioners' home had been open, he said, and he had gone in 'looking for something to steal'.

But Mr Justice Wright, having heard that Mrs Hadler

had been sexually assaulted after she was stabbed, concluded that Roberts was guilty of 'two of the most horrible murders it is possible to imagine.'

He told him, 'I have no doubt that you were driven that night by lust, inflamed by drink. When you went into that house it was because you had been unsuccessful in picking up a girl and you were looking for any woman you could find. As it was, you encountered two elderly, defenceless people and killed them both.' Roberts was jailed for life.

15

BATTERED TO DEATH

THE MURDER OF WILLIAM HOWE AT WORTHING, JANUARY 1990

Retired vet William Howe paid the ultimate price for not revealing the whereabouts of thousands of pounds worth of jewellery and valuables when he was tied up and systematically beaten at his flat in Worthing. He was tortured because he refused to tell his assailants where the safe was. Police believe at least two people were responsible for battering the 63 year old bachelor to death, but it is a crime that has never been solved.

The savage murder caused shock and disbelief in the seaside town. Mr Howe was a popular man and acclaimed as an excellent vet. Neighbours and former clients testified to his gentleness with animals and the skills which achieved full recovery in even the most hopeless-looking cases.

A homosexual, he lived alone above the surgery he used to run at 48 Victoria Road. Did he know and admit the killers to his flat that cold Monday evening of 8th January 1990? There was no evidence of a break-in; the ground floor entrance to security-conscious Mr Howe's flat was unlocked. This was so unusual that it led to the alarm being raised the following evening by fellow vet and former colleague Peter Brown, who took over the practice when Bill Howe retired. He noticed the lights

The murder victim – William Howe.

were on upstairs and on pushing the door open found objects disturbed in the hall and upstairs as if there had been a struggle and the walls 'were spattered quite liberally with blood'.

There was no sign of the silver-haired bachelor, but the door to a back bedroom was locked – and that's when Mr Brown decided to call in the police. They found the body face down on the floor, legs and arms tightly bound with electricity flex. He had been severely beaten about the head and body with both a heavy instrument – possibly a hammer – and fists. The attackers had also stamped or kneeled on the small of his back, fracturing his ribs.

The flat had been ransacked, but the killers had encountered only stony silence when they demanded to know where the safe was kept. Their victim would have been more than reluctant to tell them, not just because of

The scene of the murder in Victoria Road, Worthing.

the value of the contents but because of their considerable sentimental worth – many items had belonged to his mother and to his long-time male companion, both of whom had died the previous year. Despite the vicious beating, which left him with severe facial injuries, he bravely refused to reveal the information which would probably have saved his life. He died from asphyxia. The safe was later discovered intact by police officers, with its contents, worth tens of thousands of pounds, undisturbed. However, the intruders did escape with several costly items of personal jewellery which they snatched from the body, including a gold wedding ring, a gold wristwatch and a heavy link gold chain.

Police launched Operation Charity, the codename for the hunt for the murderers, and Mr Howe's relatives offered a £10,000 reward. Officers worked round the clock and the case was featured on the BBC's *Crimewatch* programme. The clothing of the men involved must have been covered in blood, and detectives urged people not to shield the killers.

As the weeks went by the net was widened to try to solve the puzzle. Foreign police forces were contacted and individuals from Africa, Australia and France were interviewed. Detective Inspector Graham Hill, leading the inquiry, said Mr Howe had many friends worldwide. More than a thousand people were quizzed from all over Britain in the early days of the inquiry, including Scotland and the Channel Islands. A thousand more interviews were to be carried out in the weeks that followed.

A major clue emerged in March when police released details of two sets of bloodied footprints left next to the

Shaw Taylor filming at the murder scene with Detective Inspector Graham Hill.

Killer's shoes . . . Detective Inspector Hill with footwear identical to that worn by the men the police were hunting.

vet's body. Details of the size nine Brooker basketball boots and size eight Exo-Fit training shoes were given extensive media coverage but failed to prompt a response.

Several times the murder team believed they had come tantalisingly close to a conviction. Three people were eliminated from the inquiry after being interviewed at length: a man police were seeking for an assault in the south of England who had been seen talking to friends of Mr Howe just days before the murder; another man serving a sentence for manslaughter when Mr Howe first met him; and, grotesquely, a friend who had waited for the retired vet in his flat, unaware that the body lay just feet away. He had gone to 48A Victoria Road on the afternoon of Tuesday 9th January, and found the front door open. He saw the disturbed furniture and some of the bloodstains, but assumed his friend had merely injured himself and gone to hospital. He waited for his return for some while, and was able to prove his whereabouts on the evening of the murder to detectives.

Gradually, to the intense frustration of those involved in Operation Charity, the trail ran cold. But four years later Detective Inspector Ron Chillingworth said he had not given up hope that one day the killers would be found. It was a murder mystery that proved as stubborn as the victim.

16

A TRUSTING GIRL

THE MURDER OF LORNA KING AT LITTLEHAMPTON, FEBRUARY 1991

Lorna King was a trusting sort of girl who befriended the wrong people. They systematically deceived her, cheated her and finally murdered her in repugnant circumstances.

She was in her mid-twenties and working at a Littlehampton factory. When news filtered through that her body had been found in a makeshift grave, tears were shed at Lorlin Electronics for the girl who was always cheerful. Colleague Doug Furner later recalled, 'She worked hard to make sure people were happy. Everyone loved her in the factory.' He said Lorna was a truly Christian girl. She would share a taxi with colleagues and pay for it herself. At Christmas and birthdays she always gave small gifts to her friends.

Lorna lived with her mother and stepfather at West Head, Littlehampton. She was a regular worshipper at the Wickbourne chapel and enjoyed a game of darts, playing for The Steam Packet team. Her friendly outgoing nature was to put her in the clutches of a sinister man who dabbled in the occult and a pathetic, alcoholic teenager.

Lorna wanted a flat of her own and John Merry and Andrew Stephenson, from Littlehampton's tough Clun Road council estate, got to hear about it. They befriended the 25 year old and did, indeed, help her to find a place of her own, but before moving in she was persuaded to change her correspondence address to that of unemployed Merry, 26, and his wife, Kathy. Lorna would not have realised that the couple were deeply in debt to the tune of about £6,000.

The Merrys stole cash and postal orders addressed to Lorna. They used her cheque book and guarantee card to obtain money, cheating her out of her £4,000 savings, and went on a spending spree with her building society book. They fleeced her under the guise of friendship, taking cynical advantage of the fact that Lorna seemed to have developed a girlish crush on Merry. He was later to tell a court, 'she was slow, quite childish. She acted like an 18 year old.' She sent him a note saying how pleased she was to have been invited to the couple's Christmas party, and Merry had shown it to his wife, 'It was something I would expect a teenager to do,' he said.

Lorna became a regular visitor to the couple's council flat. Hovering on the sidelines was the Merry's neighbour Stephenson, a young man with a drink problem and a regular user of cannabis and LSD. He had an IQ of only 76, which put him on the borderline of being mentally deficient. He, too, had benefited from the stolen cheque book and bank card.

It was only a matter of time before Lorna found out that her cash had been disappearing alarmingly – she had already become suspicious – and Merry was prepared to go to any lengths to escape discovery.

On the evening of Sunday, 3rd February 1991, Lorna spent the evening with Merry and his wife. Stephenson was there too, as usual, drinking heavily and smoking cannabis. Eerily, Merry performed a tarot card reading for the three of them – though Lorna's future now consisted of hours rather than years. He was fascinated by the occult. The couple owed £160 to the West Sussex County Council library service for books on the subject which had never been returned or were damaged.

The murder victim – Lorna King.

When the evening ended, Merry and Stephenson offered to walk Lorna to the taxi rank at Littlehampton railway station. Before they left the flat, Merry armed himself with a heavy wheel brace and a length of aerial cable.

Lewes Crown Court was later to hear what happened in the minutes that followed. The two men led Lorna across muddy fields to a deserted ill-lit spot at the former Littlehampton camp site, reduced to desolate wasteland by construction work on the town's bypass. Then Merry struck the victim around the head with the wheel brace while Stephenson held her down. The men dragged her 300 yards through the mud and struck her again. Merry then attempted to strangle Lorna with the cable but part of it snapped, so the pair throttled her with the remains of it. Afterwards, Merry was alleged to have said, 'The bitch wouldn't die.'

He pushed her head into a puddle of water to make sure she was dead. Then the two men stole her purse and other possessions and concealed the body in a rough grave. After returning home, Merry told Stephenson to walk his pet dog to make sure 'she had snuffed it'. Lorna's partially buried body was subsequently found by workmen on the A259 bypass construction site.

Both men blamed the other for the callous murder. Merry maintained that Stephenson wanted to ask Lorna out; he did not want a serious relationship and needed someone else present if she rejected him. Merry had hung back as the couple went through the tunnel under the railway line, got tired of waiting and started to walk home. 'Andy' came running up behind him, breathing heavily. Merry said he asked where Lorna was and his friend replied, 'She is down on the track. I think I've killed her.' Merry said Stephenson told him he had 'wandering hands and was having a good grope' when she started to object and screamed. He had slapped her when she became hysterical, Merry said he was told. Stephenson had then picked something off the ground and hit her with it. Merry advised Stephenson to go to the police and tell them it was an accident.

Stephenson had a different story. He told the court he was forced to help his neighbour Merry strangle Lorna because he feared he would be the next victim if he disagreed. Under cross-examination he broke down in tears as he admitted, 'I don't know what the truth is because I can't remember. I have been known to have an alcohol problem.'

Mr Robert Seabrook QC, prosecuting, said Stephenson had shown the police where the attack took place and where the body had been found, with no problem. 'Is it too painful to remember now, the terrible thing you did to that poor girl?'

Stephenson replied, 'I don't remember being there.'

The court heard that a heavily bloodstained pair of jeans and a leather jacket had been found at the home of Merry. A piece of aerial cable was also found in the flat, with one end still attached to the television. A black denim jacket belonging to Stephenson was heavily stained with Lorna's blood and a wheel brace found at Merry's home was also smeared with human blood.

Three drains had been searched in Clun Road by police. They found a piece of newspaper with several items wrapped inside including a Halifax Building Society book in the name of Miss L. King, a postal order torn in half and an Abbey National £50 cheque guarantee card cut into four pieces.

The jury took 24 hours to reach their unanimous verdict at the end of the eleven day trial: both men were guilty of murder. Stephenson burst into tears and Merry shook his head in disbelief.

Before sentence was passed, Stephenson's defence, Mr Michael Gayle QC, said the youth was extremely young

'A very considerable danger to anyone he crosses' . . . John Merry.

and the sort of person who was easily led. He added that he had had a disturbed upbringing after being put into care at the age of two, and had been bullied throughout his school life.

Speaking for Merry, Mr John Tanzer said the man had been under tremendous domestic pressures, but the judge, Mr Justice Buckley, said, 'He was in debt. A lot of people are in debt but they do not go around hitting innocent young girls. Anyone who heard the sheer callousness of the actions that took place would know that Merry instigated and led. He is a very considerable danger to anyone he crosses.' Sentencing the pair, he said, 'The sentence prescribed by the law for murder is one of life and that is the sentence I pass on each of you.'

Afterwards Detective Superintendent Graham Hill, who led the investigation, said Lorna King was a much-liked girl who did not deserve to die. 'She was also a trusting girl who had no idea that her money was being misused in the way it was.'

17

DEATH OF A DEALER

THE MURDER OF DEREK GOODEY AT WESTERGATE, FEBRUARY 1991

Small-time drugs dealer Derek Goodey was lured to his 'extremely bloody' death by a girlfriend. The 27 year old was smashed over the head with an axe and strangled after being invited to the home of Tessa Young, in Westergate, near Bognor Regis.

The stricken Goodey, still living, was then wrapped in bin liners and driven to the Hesworth Common beauty spot near Fittleworth. He was put in the back of his Toyota car and it was set alight. Goodey's body was burned beyond recognition and had to be identified from dental records. He had died from asphyxia.

The gruesome killing took place after plans were made by a gang to 'rip off' Goodey, who was suspected of being a police informant, for a quantity of drugs. Pretty Tessa had agreed to entice him to her council home in Ivy Lane, but could not bear to be in the same room when he was attacked. Instead, Lewes Crown Court was to hear, she stayed in the kitchen and could hear the sound of the dealer begging for his life in the living room at the front of the house. There were 'choking and gurgling noises', and she put her fingers in her ears to block out the ghastly sounds.

Goodey had been hopelessly outnumbered. Gary Brain and his common-law wife Tracey Wood were waiting in an upstairs room, while David Gibson and Nigel Wilson were lurking outside, ready to pounce on their victim when he arrived. The plot had been formulated the day before the killing in February 1991.

Things did not go to plan when Goodey arrived with a friend, but Tessa invited him to come back later on his own. With the promise of a more intimate evening in prospect, Goodey returned and Tessa opened the door to him. He was immediately set upon and the woman rushed to hide in the kitchen while her erstwhile boyfriend was bundled by the four gang members into the front room where the fatal attack took place.

After the killing the blood-stained section of carpet was cut out and later dumped beside a motorway. When new carpet was brought to the house, guilt-ridden Tessa placed a silver cross underneath it at the spot where her 'on-off' boyfriend had been bludgeoned with the axe and throttled.

The background to the killing was rooted in the shadowy world of the drugs culture. Goodey dealt in cannabis and amphetamine – as did the others in the case. He had made a deal to supply amphetamine to Brain, formerly of Bognor, in his new 'patch' in Hatfield, Hertfordshire. Shortly before the killing Brain, a mechanic, still owed thousands of pounds on the deal. He planned the 'rip off' with his four friends, all from the Bognor area and all deeply involved in the drugs world.

Brain, 21, got a life sentence for his part in the killing, as did joiner Wilson, 23. Hopeless addict Gibson was cleared of murder but convicted of manslaughter and jailed for eight years. He had told police he was so doped or drunk on the night of the killing he could not remember a thing about it.

Sentencing the three men, Mr Justice Drake said, 'This was a horrible killing and the action afterwards with attempting to burn the body so as to remove all evidence was a very grave action and horrible conduct. The fact

115

The burnt-out Toyota car in which the body of Derek Goodey was found at Hesworth Common, Fittleworth.

that the victim was not a man of good character is neither here nor there when it comes to who was guilty in taking part in his killing.'

Tracey Wood, too, was cleared of murder but convicted of manslaughter. She was a 'pathetic victim' who had fallen under the 'Svengali-like character' of her common-law husband Brain. At 27, she was the mother of five children, although one had been fostered and three more were in local care. The youngest child was being looked after by her mother, and she was again in the early weeks of pregnancy when she appeared before the court. Mr Justice Drake told her, 'Whatever you did was done very much under the evil influence of Gary Brain with whom you were living as man and wife.' He jailed her for four years.

Tessa Young, the girlfriend who helped lure Derek Goodey to his appalling death, was spared a prison sentence because her evidence helped jail the four others involved. She received merely a suspended sentence after admitting perverting the course of justice. Her plea of not guilty to murder was accepted; and she later gave evidence for the prosecution, saying she had no idea that Goodey would be killed. The judge said it had taken 'considerable courage' to testify against her former friends. He said, 'Some people might think that at the end of this case you got off very lightly indeed. That is because you co-operated with the police and gave evidence in court.'

The blonde mother of two had initially told police the bogus story that Goodey had been abducted from her home by two masked men, but when she decided to tell the truth she became the main prosecution witness. She insisted she did not know the dealer was going to be murdered that chilly February night.

'I had only been in the kitchen a matter of minutes when Dave (Gibson) was in the doorway,' she said. 'He was very white and looked in a state of shock and said to me he thought Derek was dead. I could hear Derek making choking and coughing noises. I sat on the kitchen floor opposite Dave and I remember putting my fingers in my ears.'

The gang then drove through the darkness to Hesworth Common in two cars, one of them belonging to the victim, where Goodey was incinerated. Tessa recalled, 'Tracey told me to stay in the car and lock the doors. I hunched up in the back seat. I lay down and had my eyes closed. My eyes opened with a bright light and it seemed the woods were on fire. They all came running and got into the car.'

The murder victim's father, Keith Goodey, said after the trial, 'Derek was a good kid and I shall miss him the rest of my days. It was a crying shame how he got mixed up with these people.'

18

THE RED BARON

THE MURDER OF LYNNE ROGERS AT ROTHERFIELD, SEPTEMBER 1991

Lynne Rogers was an ordinary 17-year-old who was keen to get on in life. She dreamt of a career in the travel industry and sent hundreds of CVs to travel companies hoping to get a job.

She was delighted to get a reply from a man who said he had a vacancy in an office which specialised in executive flights to Belgium, Holland and France. When she set off for an interview, her father Derek wrote her a good luck note:

Dear Lynne,
Don't forget the porch key.
Don't forget to phone me as often as possible.
Don't forget to wash behind your ears.
Love Dad, XXX

Mr Rogers never saw his daughter alive again.

He became worried on the afternoon of the interview, September 4th, 1991, after not hearing from her and decided to inform the police.

Five days later the body of the pretty, ginger-haired teenager was found hidden in a remote corner of Sussex. Farm worker John Rumens was cutting grass in the grounds of Rotherhurst, a mansion in lonely Rotherhurst Lane, one mile south of the picturesque village of

Rotherfield, when he found the girl's body dumped in brambles just yards from the edge of the road. The girl who was devoted to her family, her boyfriend Spencer Clark and to her horse Duke, had been strangled. Although her smart, interview clothes were dishevelled there was no sign of sexual assault. Curiously, there was a bite mark on her chin.

One of the biggest Sussex Police investigations for years was launched, with nearly 300 police officers searching the woods and carrying out interviews. They pieced together the last few days of Lynne's life.

On August 30th, a man had called the Rogers family home in Catford, south-east London, and spoke to her 19-year-old sister, Suzanne. He told her about the exciting job vacancy. The man rang again later in the evening and Suzanne told him to try again the next day. She could hear radio conversation in the background, as if from an air traffic control tower.

The man duly rang back and this time Lynne was at home to answer the call. Her sister saw her on the phone, making notes on a jotting pad. She scribbled: 'Charter, light air, 28,000 dollar/£14,500, 10 am, 9-5 pm.' The interview was to be at 10 am at Charing Cross railway station in London. She was to catch the 9.17 train from Hither Green.

On September 3rd, the man made his final call and an excited Lynne told her father that after the interview the next day she would be travelling by car from Charing Cross to Shoreham on the Sussex coast and then by helicopter to Gatwick. She had been told to bring her passport in case they had to fly somewhere and that they would in any case be ending up at the Hilton in London for dinner.

The persistent caller and the 'iffy job' aroused suspicion in the family, still reeling from the death of Lynne's mother six months before, but they wished her

Lynne Rogers: Lured to her death.

luck. Lynne kept her appointment at the station the next morning and a cab driver was able to provide a photofit description of the man she met there 'as if waiting for a blind date', and the car he was driving – a blue Vauxhall Carlton.

On the same day, farmer Richard Ellis had spotted a solitary man in a blue Vauxhall parked in a layby near Rotherfield.

Police knew Lynne had been job hunting and had sent her CV to a travel company called Africa Hinterland, based at the Greenwich Business Centre in London. They began interviewing the other 130 businesses operating there and stumbled on an individual called Scott Singleton, who had a car repair business called Casualty Car Doctor in unit 601. He matched their photofit description, owned a blue Vauxhall Carlton and lived in Crawley – with Gatwick airport on the doorstep.

This aroused their suspicions because of the wanted man's apparent knowledge of airports and aviation. Detective Superintendent Mike Bennison believed Singleton might have found Lynne's CV in the business centre's communal post room. The police chief then discovered that the man's girlfriend, Kim Arnold, lived within a few hundred yards of the Rogers' home.

Singleton's knowledge of aviation – he had worked at Gatwick and belonged to Stapleford Flying Club – made Bennison even more sure.

Then a vital witness came forward. David Sanderson was using a payphone near Crawley Post Office on August 31st and noticed the man in the next booth had a CV with Lynne Rogers' name on it. He was claiming to be an executive offering someone thousands of dollars to work in the travel industry. But from a payphone?

Scott Singleton was arrested but there was not enough evidence to charge him. He was released and kept under surveillance.

A picture emerged of a man who called himself The Red Baron and lived a life of fantasy, obsessed with his imaginary world of jet aircraft and jet-set women. In fact he was at 35, a short, balding, gap-toothed wheeler-dealer who lived in a council flat at Wilkinson Court, Crawley.

He left school at 16 with a basic knowledge of carpentry but told girlfriends he was a fighter pilot who had been injured in a plane crash and even showed them the scars on his chest. In fact, he inflicted them himself in an unsuccessful suicide attempt.

The dreamer claimed to be the great-great grandson of the First World War German fighter Ace, Baron Manfred von Richthofen – the Red Baron. He said he was half Belgian and half German and claimed his father disowned him when he joined the RAF.

He would dress in an airline pilot's uniform and listen to air traffic control announcements on a radio scanner. He told people he owned an aeroplane and a helicopter when all he had was a second-hand microlite. He did not even know how to fly.

Det. Supt. Bennison said: 'One girlfriend recalled how he lay on the sofa pretending to be asleep when he suddenly said, "Tango Three, Tango Three, can't eject, can't eject." Then he opened his eyes and claimed not to know anything about it.'

Singleton even convinced his estranged wife, Pat Reich, that he could fly by sitting in the co-pilot seat on a light aircraft flight to Belgium. But the pilot beside him was really in control.

Crawley divorcee Tracey Whyton recalled that he seemed obsessed with women and was always asking her out. 'He used to give me the creeps and I didn't like to be alone with him,' she said. She had made a council house swap with Singleton early in 1991 when she moved to his Crowberry Close home and he took her Wilkinson Court property nearby. She said he was paranoid and would try to find out what people thought about him by leaving tape recorders running.

She described how he read tarot cards and left a death card in the house when she moved in. She also found a stick of dynamite behind the cooker. She remembered, 'He just said "I wondered where that had got to." '

A tape of air traffic control announcements with Singleton's voice saying his 'flight call sign', Papa 101, was found at his flat; the same words the murdered girl's sister heard during one of the phone calls to their home.

It was the killer's own savagery that caused his downfall. When police turned their attention to the bite mark on Lynne's chin, Singleton refused to give a dental impression of his own teeth. But an old mould was found at O'Geary's dental surgery in Crawley which matched the marks found on the dead girl's face.

Police believe he watched Lynne, who lived close to his lover's Catford home, before dreaming up his ultimate fantasy game. Lewes Crown Court was told by Robert Seabrooke, QC, prosecuting, 'Singleton had become excited by the idea of trapping Lynne Rogers. He had a misguided idea that he could get satisfaction if he could get her under his control.'

Lynne fought off Singleton's advances and, when his dream bubble burst, he lost control and punched, bit and strangled her.

Singleton celebrated his 36th birthday standing in the dock on the first day of the trial. Before his first appearance in court he had made an unsuccessful suicide attempt during breakfast in his cell at Crawley police station. He was taken to hospital with cuts to his neck, which needed stitching.

Singleton was born in Yorkshire and christened Andre Reich. He changed his name by deed poll. He had a wife, two children and a string of convictions. He left his wife and had a number of girlfriends, picked up at petrol

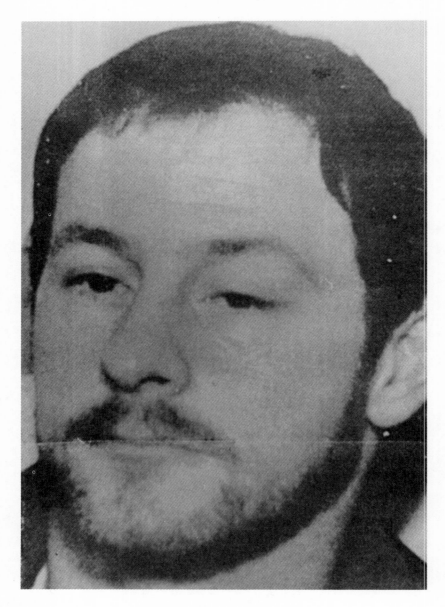

Singleton: A cruel, callous and calculating killer.

stations, in the street and even traffic jams.

Many women saw through his fantastic boasts and grew tired of him. Others went out with him so they could laugh at his fantasies. Det. Supt. Bennison said, 'He aimed for divorced women with children. Getting hold of Lynne Rogers' CV was an added bonus. He probably thought she was a young näive woman but she was worldly-wise and headstrong and wouldn't take any of his nonsense. That's perhaps why she died.'

At the end of a three-week trial during July, 1992, the jury found The Red Baron guilty of murder and he was jailed for life. As Singleton was led to the cells, Lynne's heartbroken father Derek lunged at him screaming: 'I will kill you. I will kill you, by God. I will have you one way or the other.'

He then shouted, 'Life? Is that all he got after all he's done to my family and my daughter?'

Mr Rogers was ordered to leave the court and his daughter Suzanne fled in tears.

Almost two years later Singleton lost his appeal against conviction. He claimed the dental records obtained by the police should not have been allowed in evidence without his consent. But Lord Justice Farquharson ruled that as the records were given voluntarily by the dentist they were admissible evidence, and added that dental information often forms vital evidence in criminal investigations. He refused Singleton leave to appeal to the House of Lords.

During the hearing, Mr Rogers again lunged towards Singleton and had to be restrained. He said, 'I hope he rots in jail. I won't ever forgive him, whether he admits it or not. I want him dead. It is all I think about.'

Index